SPECTACULAR HOMES
of Western Canada

AN EXCLUSIVE SHOWCASE OF WESTERN CANADA'S FINEST DESIGNERS

Published by

Panache Partners Canada Inc.
1424 Gables Court
Plano, TX 75075
469.246.6060
Fax: 469.246.6062
www.panache.com

Publishers: Brian G. Carabet and John A. Shand

Printed in Malaysia

Distributed by Independent Publishers Group
800.888.4741

PUBLISHER'S DATA

Spectacular Homes of Western Canada

Library of Congress Control Number: 2008936705

ISBN 13: 978-1-933415-71-0
ISBN 10: 1-933415-71-1

First Printing 2009

10 9 8 7 6 5 4 3 2 1

Right: FNDA Architecture Inc, *page 145*

Previous Page: Monica Stevens Interior Design, *page 43*

This publication is intended to showcase some of the region's finest
interior designers. The publisher does not require, warrant, endorse,
or verify any professional accreditations, educational backgrounds
or professional affiliations of the individuals or firms included herein.
All copy and photography published herein has been reviewed and
approved as free of any usage fees or rights and accurate by the
individuals and/or firms included herein.

Panache Partners, LLC, is dedicated to the restoration and conservation
of the environment. Our books are manufactured using paper from mills
certified to derive their products from environmentally managed forests.
We are committed to continued investigation of alternative paper
products and environmentally responsible manufacturing processes to
ensure the preservation of our fragile planet.

SPECTACULAR HOMES
of Western Canada

AN EXCLUSIVE SHOWCASE OF WESTERN CANADA'S FINEST DESIGNERS

Bob's Your Uncle Design, Ltd, *page 59*

INTRODUCTION

Van Sickle Design Consultants Inc, *page 189*

Along the slopes of Whistler, amid the clamoring arts district of Edmonton and between the Pacific waters and coastal mountains of Vancouver, Western Canada is alive with sights and sounds that undoubtedly influence those who happily reside among such diversity. With a blend of natural and cultural ingredients, interior designers are challenged to incorporate this character and life into the residences they design. Whether in the spirited Old West that lingers on the streets of Calgary or near the junction of the Red and Assiniboine Rivers in Winnipeg, the established designers on the following pages revel in the opportunity to merge the indoors with surrounding nature—all while synthesizing the characteristics of those who have called upon them for their expertise and insight.

McIntyre Bills, *page 23*

Though the regions that comprise Western Canada are varied and reflect distinctively historical attributes, a balance of both traditional and modern aesthetics can be found. Where the natural palette is more subdued, fabrics and abundant lighting give a brighter home experience—and where the city bustles with chic, urban living quarters, pared-down furniture and downtown views are on call. It is a respect for fresh concepts—within both traditional and modern settings—that liberates these visionary designers and guides them toward solutions that continually define tomorrow's standard.

Brian Carabet and John Shand
Publishers

Ledingham Design Consultants, *page 123*

LMF International
Interior Design Consultants, Inc., *page 87*

Karen West Design Group, Inc., *page 197*

Contents

Ingenium Design Group Inc., page 29

ALBERTA & MANITOBA

JACQUELINE COREA
REENA SOTROPA

COREA SOTROPA INTERIOR DESIGN

Based in the bustling, and albeit relatively young city of Calgary, Corea Sotropa Interior Design has found its niche in applying a fair dose of bright colour to the area's interior design. Principals Reena Sotropa and Jacqueline Corea met while in design school and found that their combined similarities and differences could offer a new approach to interiors. When they first entered the scene in Calgary more than a decade ago, Reena and Jacqueline found that the status quo of most residences involved an uninviting dose of dark and masculine colours. Their fresh and undoubtedly happier approach to design has caused the firm to stand out from the rest—clients often will seek out Reena and Jacqueline's expertise for their decidedly different approach.

One look at their interiors and it's easy to identify a few hallmarks of the firm: generous portions of natural light, colourful expressions and flexibility. These attributes are further enhanced by a varied group of generally well-traveled homeowners. The area's youth and vitality is matched by clients' eagerness to incorporate international

pieces they've collected during their journeys. Reena and Jacqueline also recognize that interiors can have a youthfulness within them that travels through the years. Since many families are listed among their clientele, Reena and Jacqueline ensure these interiors are both beautiful and practical. After working with clients, reviewing magazine clippings, fabric swatches, etc., the principals are able to concentrate and mold a project's design that is indicative of their clients' lifestyles, while also leading them into current design choices.

Having worked in corporate design—a field that both principals agree is quite a departure from home interiors—Reena and Jacqueline eagerly absorb all the intricacies and more personal aspects to designing a residence. Watching their clients as they first walk into a completed home is quite possibly the most rewarding aspect—the relationships sometimes even evolve into meaningful friendships past the completion of a project. These same clients are usually the first to recommend friends and family to the professional, fun and approachable designers at Corea Sotropa Interior Design.

TOP LEFT
This fun family space is located in the basement level of the home. Several techniques were employed to create this decidedly "un-basement like" look including layered lighting, ceiling development and bright colours. The drape in the foreground was included to obscure the children's play zone and provide a pleasing backdrop to the media area.
Photograph by Leah Brandt

BOTTOM LEFT
The punchy coral and lime-green accent colours are the highlight of this combination living/dining room, which features loads of sumptuous fabrics and custom furniture.
Photograph by John Gaucher

FACING PAGE
This traditional Craftsman kitchen was inspired by the very specific aesthetic of the English architects Greene & Greene. Although this historical style was at the forefront of the design, the kitchen has all the modern conveniences in appliances, layout and finishes. The rosewood inlays and joinery details add to the Craftsman appeal.
Photograph by John Gaucher

LILLIAS COWPER

LEGATO DESIGN

Before investing a decade of her life into the lives of her children, Lillias Cowper spent her time expanding her commercial interior design portfolio. Upon returning to the workforce from her reprieve, Lillias knew that shifting to residential design offered a unique opportunity to enhance her clients' lives while utilizing her architectural background. Today, her work often revolves around renovations, redefining spaces and space planning. Focusing on what is fondly known as the heart of the home, Lillias doesn't just give kitchens new cabinets and a coat of paint. Rather, she explores the functionality of the space, and often a whole new life pulse is incorporated within its architectural reconfiguration.

Over the past decade, the kitchen's overall perception has shifted—it is now a central place for eating and engaging in conversation. The art of food preparation is also now considered sophisticated entertainment; the kitchen is no longer considered a separate entity from other home spaces, but rather an important part of everyday living. With these new emphases, homeowners are eagerly seeking Lillias for complete renovations so that their kitchens can become a cohesive part of their homes.

No matter the style employed, Lillias incorporates clean lines into every design through architectural features. She also takes advantage of surrounding exterior elements through her designs since often a home's orientation is inappropriate for its site: Windows across a back wall not only improve the view while washing dishes in a kitchen, but they can also dramatically alter the natural light that filters through other areas within the home. Along with these architectural solutions, Lillias guides her clients to consider the functionality of traditional kitchen attributes such as cabinetry—many of her kitchens will have no upper cupboards to facilitate more light and space within the room. Her comprehensive architectural solutions often flow past the kitchen and into other areas of the home as well, offering homeowners a chance to infuse a new functionality into their living and resting areas.

ABOVE
The elegantly shaped grand piano bulkhead and island is juxtaposed with the practical slate flooring, copper hood fan and rich wood cabinetry.
Photograph by Sean Dennie, www.photoganda.ca

FACING PAGE
The architectural elements of the fireplace interplay with the natural lines and textures in the artwork, carpet and cut wood pieces in the coffee table.
Photograph by Sean Dennie, www.photoganda.ca

Her clients' diverse requests are always an exciting challenge. From a kitchen with 17 appliances to specialized drawer microwaves and steamers, Lillias is always finding a creative way to meet a homeowner's needs. Once a client's home remodel required the removal of more than 55 truckloads of debris, and upon completion, the existing house had porcelain washbasins, butcher blocks and even an old stove, all of which were restored and incorporated into the new home. With thanks to modern technology, Lillias collaborates with clients in Holland, the United States and British Columbia as well, and finds these diverse regions offer an array of opportunities and challenges to further expand her creativity and design approaches.

As an extension of her work with home design, Lillias uses her education in fine art to paint watercolors for her clients and friends. She recognizes a home's emotional significance and savors the opportunity to paint watercolor portraits of certain residences. It is this love of artistry that has driven the principal of Legato Design since 1996. By remaining independent, she has no vested interest in any local manufacturers—her loyalties remain with homeowners and the creativity of the space. She sources from the artisans who can get the job done with excellence and precision, allowing her to focus on a kitchen's function and flair.

TOP LEFT
Seating takes advantage of the natural light and views. Cabinetry supports family board games including a drop-down table and chaise lounge for nighttime reading.
Photograph by Sean Dennie, www.photoganda.ca

BOTTOM LEFT
Family room casualness is enhanced with artwork and warm colours. Conversation areas are created with soft, durable upholstered bar stools and both sectional and chaise lounge seating.
Photograph by Sean Dennie, www.photoganda.ca

FACING PAGE TOP
By removing walls and redefining spaces, the kitchen now flows into the dining room, providing space for a grand piano-shaped island.
Photograph by Taryn Jollimore, www.takeonephoto.com

FACING PAGE BOTTOM
The kitchen and family room flow together with planning changes, matching natural cherry cabinetry and balancing repeated dark cherry elements.
Photograph by Taryn Jollimore, www.takeonephoto.com

Douglas Cridland

DOUGLAS CRIDLAND INTERIOR DESIGN

At heart, Douglas Cridland is a classicist drawn to symmetry. As a leader in the world of interior design for nearly three decades, he has always been drawn to strong colours, unique symmetry and mid-century furniture mixed with more traditional pieces. Using the juxtaposition of these elements and more, Douglas delights in redefining how these features can cohabitate within a room. By mixing and combining period furniture—and cleverly matching neutral palettes with stunning artwork—he uses natural products and approaches whenever possible to create unique interior spaces.

During their first meeting together, Douglas discusses many aspects that will influence his clients' lifestyles within particular spaces. And since most of his clients are working with him on second or third homes, Douglas already has a general idea of basic living preferences. What becomes important in these homes is their function, how entertaining affects spatial arrangements and how residents will live in the space.

Often times, Douglas finds that a specific colour, carpet or accessory will inspire the entire direction of a new project. Even after his many years of designing, Douglas still finds these processes exhilarating. The constant evolution of the industry makes every day exciting. In fact, he says the lack of structure contributes to the constant spark of creativity and invention.

ABOVE
Art plays an important role in the look and feel of any space. The contemporary Kristian Eckhar painting is juxtaposed with a stunning Murano chandelier from a Venice hotel.
Photograph by Robert Lemermeyer

FACING PAGE
The family room is a study in textures and neutrals; rich woodwork, contemporary carpet and artwork lend an air of relaxed sophistication.
Photograph by Robert Lemermeyer

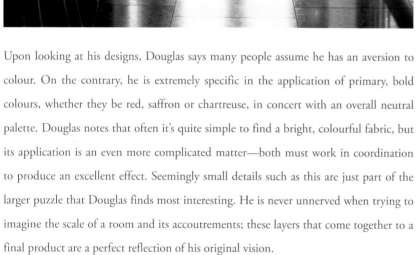

Upon looking at his designs, Douglas says many people assume he has an aversion to colour. On the contrary, he is extremely specific in the application of primary, bold colours, whether they be red, saffron or chartreuse, in concert with an overall neutral palette. Douglas notes that often it's quite simple to find a bright, colourful fabric, but its application is an even more complicated matter—both must work in coordination to produce an excellent effect. Seemingly small details such as this are just part of the larger puzzle that Douglas finds most interesting. He is never unnerved when trying to imagine the scale of a room and its accoutrements; these layers that come together to a final product are a perfect reflection of his original vision.

Since his early days as an interior designer, Douglas has been fascinated by the strong personal interaction with a client's sense of style and translation. Douglas has led his firm with style, open communication, honesty and fairness; the longevity and success of Douglas Cridland Interior Design is a clear indication of his leadership and design

savvy. By allowing his clients' unique and often challenging ideas to stretch his creative direction, Douglas can focus on what's at the heart of all his home designs. Douglas doesn't simply apply pretty furnishings; by emphasizing interiors that speak to their owners, he creates lifestyles—one room at a time.

ABOVE LEFT
Natural light, a smart layout and beautiful finishes define the kitchen and morning room, both with views of the rear gardens and Elbow River.
Photograph by Robert Lemermeyer

ABOVE RIGHT
Beyond this space an anteroom to the family is used for cards, intimate dinners and a central bar at formal and informal cocktail parties.
Photograph by Robert Lemermeyer

FACING PAGE
Attention to classical proportions is evident in this grand hall, which showcases a wall of glass with views onto a walled court and reflecting pool.
Photograph by Robert Lemermeyer

JAMES MCINTYRE
RONALD BILLS

MCINTYRE BILLS

When James McIntyre and Ronald Bills met in design school, they knew a dynamic partnership had been forged. Thanks to Ronald's natural eye for architectural detailing and James' intuitive décor sensibilities, they formed McIntyre Bills to offer clients comprehensive residential design. Although they enjoy the varied facets within interior design, it is undoubtedly a benefit to have their individual strengths contributing to each project.

Choosing a home for the design firm was simple, and Calgary's entrepreneurial spirit has only further enhanced the principals' forward-thinking creativity. Watching the city grow over the past two decades has made James and Ronald feel fortunate—the city has developed into an international destination, and the greatest clients seem to naturally find their way to the front steps of the studio. Similar to a new frontier, the city is brimming with clients who are excited about new ideas in design and who readily open the pathway so their creative processes can flourish. To put it simply, the job of designer is made even more enjoyable because Calgary residents are not followers; they lead and grow because of their open-minded personalities. Combine enthusiastic clients with visionary designers, and the process is nothing short of a remarkable journey through the world of interior design. Since establishing the firm, James and Ronald's market has broadened to include astute clientele across North America, including Victoria, Vancouver and various cities throughout California and Oregon as well.

ABOVE & FACING PAGE
Placed at the center of a 100-year-old Victoria residence is its dining room. Hand-painted wallpaper from Stark and an antique, hand-blown chandelier complement the space. Bringing further harmony to its historicity are antique French sideboards and a French gold honeycomb mirror.
Photographs by Colin Way, www.colinway.com

James and Ronald work with their style-forward and independent clientele by involving them throughout the entire design process. While Ronald focuses in the studio on interior architectural detailing, James accompanies their clients to various design showrooms. Together they travel to New York, Chicago and Los Angeles, which not only makes choosing the perfect artwork or foyer piece exciting, it also provides a stronger connection with the completed house when a memory is attached with such items. The designers realize that a stage is being set for their clients' lives—such a task is taken seriously, but when done right, it's a lot of fun along the way. After searching through showrooms all day, there's nothing James enjoys more than sipping a glass of wine with his clients and discussing the items to be acquired. In the end, the best projects are the ones where everyone remembers to have a great time.

ABOVE LEFT
A sunny guest suite serves as the perfect retreat with an antique Persian rug from England and comfortable linen covered chairs.
Photograph by Colin Way, www.colinway.com

ABOVE RIGHT
A renovated kitchen was designed for its gourmet owner. The exposed brick chimney adds character along with stained mahogany cabinets and an elegant Venetian glass chandelier.
Photograph by Colin Way, www.colinway.com

FACING PAGE
A most beloved breakfast room overlooking the residence's pool is filled with an old English collection of mismatched objects. The antique iron and porcelain chandelier adds a bit of whimsy to the space.
Photograph by Colin Way, www.colinway.com

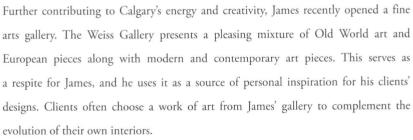

Further contributing to Calgary's energy and creativity, James recently opened a fine arts gallery. The Weiss Gallery presents a pleasing mixture of Old World art and European pieces along with modern and contemporary art pieces. This serves as a respite for James, and he uses it as a source of personal inspiration for his clients' designs. Clients often choose a work of art from James' gallery to complement the evolution of their own interiors.

Although James and Ronald's style maintains itself within contemporary flavors, the designers often create many hybrids of both modern and traditional styles; as a sign of the time, design often nods to the past while looking to the future. Overall, James and Ronald see themselves as a catalyst for their clients' dreams—client-focused choices naturally produce interiors that please everyone.

ABOVE LEFT
Restored stained glass flanks the transition space along the main stairwell. The carpet runner was custom designed to appear original with the house.
Photograph by Colin Way, www.colinway.com

ABOVE RIGHT
A chinois table from John Boone sits in front of a crushed velvet sofa, providing the largest room of the home a cozy corner. Antique ceramic and gold lamps add interest to the space.
Photograph by Colin Way, www.colinway.com

FACING PAGE
A decidedly masculine and moody men's lounge makes for a quiet spot to smoke a cigar and enjoy some 40-year-old Port.
Photograph by Colin Way, www.colinway.com

ANDREA RAIMONDI

INGENIUM DESIGN GROUP INC.

After more than a decade as an interior designer, the principal of Ingenium Design Group, Andrea Raimondi, has only one problem left to solve: how to fit nearly 10 industry accreditations and licenses onto a business card. But seeing the success of her interiors and the proliferation of her firm—which she affectionately calls the biggest little design firm in the world—Andrea continues to separate herself from the competition in each subsequent project she designs. Her youthful face may cause clients at first to second-guess the truthfulness behind Andrea's age, but once they set foot in her office, it's apparent that nothing but the best emerges from this talented designer. Named among the top 20 of the next wave of hottest designers by *Canadian House & Home*, Andrea says her earliest memories of design can be traced back to the time she spent with her father.

If she ever had a free day, Andrea could be found searching through samples and models at her father's office. An architect, Andrea's father welcomed her into the world of architecture and design, and everything that followed these first impressions is history. She had been acquainted with design from her earliest recollection—being a third-generation designer—and was engulfed in the myriad aspects that relate to interiors from a young age. Rather than simply educating herself on the principles of interior design, she began working on various projects in many levels. Although her father worked mainly in the commercial and construction aspects of design, Andrea still enjoys conversing with him and gleaning his broad range of viewpoints.

Upon completing her schooling, she gained invaluable experience as an interior designer before founding Ingenium Design Group in 2000. The firm is based in Calgary, and its varied work is a direct reflection of the city's expanding international mélange. To stay in tune with such a diverse set of clients and their respective needs, Andrea places a strong value on allowing travel to function as a research avenue. For a rustic retreat, she may travel to Aspen or for a boutique hotel, she has been known to journey to Europe. There's no limit to the knowledge that can be gained when Andrea is immersed in a new culture—and the proof is evident not only in the final product but her clients' satisfaction. As her client base expands, so too does her portfolio, which includes suburban residential projects, resorts, inner city penthouses, restaurants and more.

While she's known for pushing the envelope in every aspect of her designs, Andrea offers an assortment of creative outlets. Design features of a recent penthouse project included coil drapery partitions, Moooi lighting, Philippe Starck plumbing fixtures as well as extensive glass inserts and stainless-steel detailing. The inspiration for such modern and unique additions rests among a multitude of thoughts and experiences that Andrea draws upon when envisioning her projects—each one is a new chance to grow.

ABOVE
The kitchen area demonstrates the gallery of finishes from the intensely saturated high-gloss orange cabinets, back-painted white glass doors through to the dynamic stainless-steel detailing. The glass and resin accents combine to create the sparkle of the reflective areas.
Photograph by Ingenium Design Group Inc.

FACING PAGE
The living room follows the austere look throughout but boasts rare pieces of furniture and art. Featured on the largest wall is an original Marcel Barbeau, from which the room gains its dynamic colours. A handcrafted baby grand Steinway piano is opposite a highly polished aluminum chair.
Photograph by Ingenium Design Group Inc.

Always searching for a new avenue to explore creatively, Andrea and her team of designers are never intimidated—even when they don't speak a client's language. Rather than seeing such a difference as an obstacle, they see it as a chance to design in a new culture. Inspiration for these buildings is often drawn from media, industrial design and even fashion runways in Europe. By looking at the artful and creative industries as a whole, the firm pulls influences from these progressive outlets and allows them to inform each design.

ABOVE LEFT
The niche's detail is complemented by the cantilevered high-gloss white cabinets.
Photograph by Ingenium Design Group Inc.

ABOVE RIGHT
From a secret stainless paneled wall into the elevator entry hallway, the three-dimensional high-gloss wall paneling integrates with LED square inserts currently shown in the blue spectrum. A water feature illuminates the elevation at the end.
Photograph by Ingenium Design Group Inc.

FACING PAGE TOP
Orange resin doors divide the master suite and the ensuite. The master bedroom showcases the custom white leather and stainless headboard.
Photograph by Ingenium Design Group Inc.

FACING PAGE BOTTOM
Looking through to the ensuite the glass-framed freestanding tub, chromotherapy rain dome and Philippe Starck fixtures integrate the sophisticated with the modern spa detailing. Embedded behind the mirror is an unexpected television, unique and unrevealed until activated.
Photograph by Ingenium Design Group Inc.

Upon completion of a project, Andrea takes the greatest satisfaction knowing that every possible need of the client has been met. Such similar sentiments have been echoed through her clients over the years: When they receive the keys to their new home, every item is in place, from art to wine. Often, a client's interaction with Andrea and her team is limited—a very special kind of trust is established from the start of any project. As a byproduct of this relationship, the designer receives freedom to create with the guidance of the client's needs. Ask Andrea which is her favorite part of design and she'll instinctively explain her love of its multifaceted demands. Design isn't just about one single detail or paint shade. It is the artful combination of a multitude of elements so that they surprise and redefine interior design.

KIM SCHROEDER

CHARISMA, THE DESIGN EXPERIENCE

Kim Schroeder, BID, once heard that "an effective living space enhances your lifestyle, soothes the spirit and delights the eye." Espousing this philosophy, she has dedicated her career to creating architectural interiors for private residences, award-winning model homes and commercial projects.

It was when her parents built a home that Kim first pored over their design books, imagining what the spaces would look like—she knew from the age of 12 that she would become an interior designer. Upon graduating from the University of Manitoba, Kim received the gold medal in interior design, and soon after launched her full service interior design firm, Charisma.

Holding to her firm's slogan as "the design experience," Kim takes a concept-to-completion approach with each project—she and her team undertake everything from the architecturally styled conceptual phase of a space to the fully constructed, furnished

and provisioned interior. At the start of any project, Kim relies on her unique ability to listen and read between the lines when reviewing the client's needs and preferences. Often she asks clients to complete the "Getting to Know You" questionnaire—designed by Charisma—and to collect photographs of spaces they find appealing. By looking at their collection of photos, she can detect the pattern of features that they might have been unable to express in words.

ABOVE
With varying heights and depths, this vanity is complete with a round vessel sink, make-up area and ample storage.
Photograph courtesy of Charisma, the design experience

FACING PAGE
Upon replacing the old dining room with a new kitchen, this space now features a compass star in luxury vinyl tile, quartz countertops and a metal laminate backsplash.
Photograph by Steve Salnikowski, Chronic Creative

Kim stresses that completed projects should not reflect her or Charisma's personality, but her clients'. As such, significant research is involved to develop the suitable character or style that is reflected in the preliminary layout and sketches. In the next phase, working drawings include space planning, architectural detailing, lighting designs, millwork and material specifications, all of which are incorporated in accordance to the unique needs and particular style of each client. With every phase, the client's input is very important.

After careful assembly of the architectural elements, the designer proceeds to the selection of furniture, window coverings and accessories. All decisions are made in consultation with the client to ensure the space is highly personalized. Subsequently, during the construction phase, Kim provides on-site supervision to ensure the realization of each design element.

Kim notes that design is a careful process—at times, it's a patient search for the right solution, rather than a prolific brain wave. When interest was lagging in the one-bedroom suites within a condominium conversion project, Kim was posed with a unique challenge. After careful analysis of the market, she completed a model suite, and within one month, the units were completely sold. It is these kinds of winning solutions that have contributed to the firm's success. Each client receives the uncompromising attention to detail and personal style upon which Charisma has built its reputation.

TOP RIGHT
The huge barrel-vaulted ceiling, bulkheads with indirect lighting and custom-built two-sided fireplace wall complement the unique art collection.
Photograph by Rusty Barton

BOTTOM RIGHT
The media wall—made of a combination of lyptus wood and distressed faux leather—creates the focal point with creative art behind the projection screen and shelves for the sculpture collection.
Photograph by Rusty Barton

FACING PAGE TOP
Unique lighting mimics the rectangular ceiling details. Deep crimson walls create a warm and inviting dining space.
Photograph by Rusty Barton

FACING PAGE BOTTOM
This new home features exquisite drywall ceiling details, lyptus cabinets, charcoal-stained maple floors and an iridescent glass tile backsplash.
Photograph by Rusty Barton

More than two decades after establishing her firm, Kim continues to engage in projects of all scopes and magnitudes. She has a reputable team of dedicated professionals including architects, engineers and builders to call upon as each project requires. Whether commissioned for residential or commercial, new construction or renovation, the Charisma team forges special, lasting relationships with clients while designing interiors that inspire.

TOP RIGHT
A new island transforms this kitchen and complements the pewter metallic laminate cabinets, granite countertops, metal laminate backsplash and unique track lighting.
Photograph courtesy of Charisma, the design experience

BOTTOM RIGHT
Rift-cut maple and stainless-steel cabinets, granite countertops and slate tile, along with unique wall niches create this unique main bathroom.
Photograph by Doug Dealey, Dealey Photographic Services

FACING PAGE TOP
The renovated space features antique carved columns, amazing tile work on the face of the bar and fan hood, while the creative lighting and niches feature the art collection.
Photograph by Michael Roberts, Duality Photographic

FACING PAGE BOTTOM
This outdoor seating area is void of insects thanks to a polycarbonate ceiling, which still allows natural light to flood the space and illuminate the stone wall. The slip-covered furniture is extremely comfortable.
Photograph by Kim Schroeder

MONICA STEVENS

MONICA STEVENS INTERIOR DESIGN

With a career spanning more than two decades and her namesake firm that was founded in 1990, Monica Stevens can look back over her life and firmly say that all roads led her to a life of design. Monica holds an honors bachelor's degree in interior design and is a professional member of the Interior Designers of Canada. Since the inception of her firm, her talent and experience have brought both national and international projects.

Today she engages talent from a group of artisans, craftsmen, architects and engineers, and enjoys the process of problem-solving with such creative individuals. But before pen is put to paper, Monica invests a significant amount of time in learning and developing a relationship with her clients. Because she is acutely aware that her clients must feel a sense of belonging and ownership during the design process, Monica listens to their needs and integrates their requirements into the final plans.

One such requirement is a sense of personalization, which often hinges on the selection of art. In one of Monica's projects, her client searched out an old Indian ceremonial dress for her home that rests within a western mountain setting—and it couldn't have been more perfect for the home's location. This same client also worked with Monica on a previous French Country home where she personalized the space by contributing a beautiful, antique 10-foot tapestry from England. In every project, it is Monica's goal to integrate good art with well-planned interiors so each home has a unique flavor that reflects the clients' personalities.

ABOVE
The entry features a custom-designed steel, nickel and granite console table, which is paired with a stunning painting by West Coast painter Takao Tanabe. A custom zebrano wood cocktail table with a vintage glass vase came from Circa, and the sofa and chairs are Le Jules Verne and upholstered in John Hutton Lounge Lizard. The black copper, African-inspired Tessa floor lamp is from McGuire Furniture.
Photograph by Colin Way Photography, www.colinway.com

FACING PAGE
Geoffrey Hunter's *Blue Sky* presides over a seating area. Together with Donald Stinson's organic shaped burled wood bowl, the two pieces create a dramatic visual of texture and colour.
Photograph by Colin Way Photography, www.colinway.com

For nearly two decades, Monica has established her reputation on designing comfortable, elegant and sensual interiors that are driven by quality. Her keen attention to detail and use of the finest materials are impeccably matched with a renowned simplicity of execution. Working with both modern and traditional vernaculars has been a particular highlight for Monica, who finds the mixture of both styles produces the most successful interiors. The elegance that is achieved through this juxtaposition of materials is one of the many reasons clients continue to enjoy working with her on more than one home. Such a compliment is reflective of not just her design intuition, but also that homeowners appreciate having Monica influence the manner in which they live their lives.

Throughout her many journeys in the world of interior design, Monica finds that her work is consistently inspired by the simple, classic execution of materials, which forever enhances every client's way of life. Quite simply, she has defined the quintessential approach to creating homes of unmatched intelligence and purpose.

LINDA TRENHOLM

LINDA TRENHOLM DESIGN INC.

Whether it was drawing classes or pottery lessons, Linda Trenholm always had a passion for creative expression. Working as a flight attendant for more than two decades enabled Linda to travel the world extensively. During her extended stays overseas she developed a love for design and architecture; this exposure led her to reconsider the path she was on. In order to immerse herself in a career that would utilize both her creativity and eye for detail on a day-to-day basis, Linda returned to school and earned a degree in interior design.

Inspired by elements in nature, Linda loves the simplistic essence that emerges from organic materials. For Linda, it's all about contrast; she loves the tension that is created by mixing a sleek material such as glass with an organic, rough finish such as stone. Regardless of the style—whether it be a richly traditional home or a modern urban boutique hotel—she is drawn to clean lines and the incorporation of natural stones, woods and textures.

LEFT
The study was driven by the concept of creating a gentleman's quarters. Dark rich woods, plush wool carpet and the crackling of a fire in the oversized fireplace create the perfect setting to unwind, play a game of pool or sip on a fine scotch after a long day.
Photograph by John Gaucher

On occasion, if she finds that her inspirations need renewal, the first place Linda returns to is nature. The textures within the Earth or even the natural shimmer of water often invoke specific designs in her mind. Linda believes that anything that looks right in an organic setting can look spectacular in an applied finish. Perfect proportion and balance can always be found when searching beyond the face value of nature.

Translating these experiences and interactions into a home's design varies from client to client. While she agrees that her designs maintain a certain aesthetic, her focus remains with the individual needs and tastes of each client. Once Linda has established the structure and finishes of a home, her associate carries on her vision and infuses the home with unique décor.

In addition to her design work, Linda also writes a design trends column for the Alberta-based *Renovations Magazine*. By offering informative design solutions, her scope of influence is expanded, helping her readers enhance their surroundings. This positive attitude is one that continues to guide Linda's adventures through interior design—she simply loves helping people improve their environments.

ABOVE LEFT
Inspired by function, the mudroom was designed to accommodate the needs of a large family living on acreage. Custom millwork not only provides storage for everything from hockey equipment to gardening supplies but gives the space a sense of serenity.
Photograph by John Gaucher

ABOVE TOP
This family room was designed as a space to relax with family and friends. Traditional architectural elements, such as the handcrafted windows and custom millwork coupled with the casual furnishings, generate a sense of comfort and unity for a large family.
Photograph by John Gaucher

ABOVE BOTTOM
An oversized island and the combination of natural colours and plenty of windows all contribute to defining this space as the heart of the home. A mixture of traditional design elements such as the coffered ceiling and fresh, bright colours create a timeless look and feel.
Photograph by John Gaucher

FACING PAGE
Designed for a bachelor with a passion for travel, this living room combines a scotch bar and an extensive built-in library wall to display all the treasures of traveling. Both tactile and sensual, textures ranging from velvet and silk furnishings to the reclaimed wood of the rugged dining table are sure to appeal to the senses.
Photograph by John Bilodeau

Mitchell Freedland Design, *page 101*

BRITISH COLUMBIA

CATHERINE ADAMS

CATHERINE ADAMS INTERIORS

Her work has been described as innovative and culturally inclusive, and Catherine Adams couldn't be more pleased. Within every project, extra time is invested to explore and understand clients' cultural intricacies—an aspect that interior designers often overlook. Tapping into their historical backgrounds is crucial to her designs, and the cohesive ambience within each new space is unmistakable. Catherine's designs exude a comfort and stability, and always weave the client's essence into the smallest details. In general, European, Asian and Caribbean influences can be detected within her designs, but upon completion, whether it is a kitchen or commercial office renovation, clients often find themselves reflected in even the tiniest nook and cranny.

Working with a diverse clientele provides endless challenges and opportunities for the design team at Catherine Adams Interiors. The relaxed lifestyle that Vancouver offers, and its diverse international residents, combines to reflect the unique Canadian West Coast in CAI's impressive body of work. A recent project illustrates the liberated and more contemporary side of Vancouverites: Instead of typical drywall, an engineering firm's office features tile, marble and granite on both its walls and floors. While it is a departure from the conservative styles of most residents, this state-of-the-art building effectively uses clean, simple and modern designs and an architecturally intriguing floorplan. From a commercial standpoint, Catherine understands the importance of identifying her clients' target market and accordingly creates environments where sales are measurably enhanced.

ABOVE
This wine cellar was designed to create an Old World atmosphere with a touch of contemporary elegance.
Photograph by Ivan Hunter Photography

FACING PAGE
A warm and inviting welcome to this West Coast-inspired dining space fuses the outdoor elements inside.
Photograph by Ivan Hunter Photography

Synthesizing the numerous personalities and backgrounds of her clientele is no easy task, and Catherine finds that traveling keeps her perspectives fresh, current and relevant. In fact, extensive international excursions through Southeast Asia served as the catalyst for her interior design career. After taking a course in interior design and discovering a sincere passion for the industry, Catherine studied at BCIT and received her accreditation in the United States, but still says that traveling was her greatest education. Citing Spain's eclectic blend of modern buildings within an Old World atmosphere, she recognizes the impact of each city's religious, cultural and architectural layers and uses similar elements in her designs.

ABOVE LEFT
This modern, yet eclectic space was inspired by the use of Makassar ebony, limestone and textured faux leather wall covering to try and blend the eras of Southeast Asian and classical yet modern design.
Photograph by Ivan Hunter Photography

ABOVE TOP
Ledgestone and limestone details along with contemporary furnishings facilitate a cozy ambience in this secondary living space.
Photograph by Ivan Hunter Photography

ABOVE BOTTOM
Limestone columns and simple cabinetry decrease visual noise and give a feeling of spaciousness in this penthouse kitchen.
Photograph by Ema Peter Photography

FACING PAGE TOP
Casual elegance is achieved using both warm and cool neutrals, while visual tensions leave the space feeling calm yet lively.
Photograph by Ema Peter Photography

FACING PAGE BOTTOM
A modern bedroom offers a quiet retreat through a neutral palette and warm textures.
Photograph by Ema Peter Photography

At the end of each project, Catherine finds great satisfaction when she sees her clients' positive reactions. Many choose to express their gratitude through a letter, and their thoughts all contain the same sentiments—designing a space with Catherine Adams Interiors is not just a task, it is a journey to finding oneself.

TOP RIGHT
The use of Makassar ebony in this ensuite creates a paradox between modern and classical elements with the use of silver leaf framing, crown moulding and jewel-like lighting.
Photograph by Ivan Hunter Photography

BOTTOM RIGHT
This elegant bedroom is dressed with an opalino glass chandelier from Venice, Italy, and also utilizes a mixture of textures and subtle changes in colour to create a modern yet elegant space.
Photograph by Ivan Hunter Photography

FACING PAGE
West Coast, Old World and Southeast Asian elements were cohesively fused to create an open, eclectic and multifunctional space.
Photograph by Ivan Hunter Photography

ADA BONINI
CHERYL BROADHEAD

BOB'S YOUR UNCLE DESIGN, LTD

Curious prospective clients might take a second look at Bob's Your Uncle Design merely for its eccentric name, and principals Cheryl Broadhead, RID, and Ada Bonini, RID, say that Bob does his job well. Derived from a British catchphrase, some say the phrase "Bob's your uncle" originates from the late 1800s when Lord Robert Cecil Salisbury was Prime Minister. After bestowing a number of positions on an unpopular nephew, having an "Uncle Bob" was soon equated with unquestionable success.

With years of experience in the interior design industry, Cheryl and Ada have established BYU Design as a fresh and innovative interior design company that strives to produce harmonious spaces that excite. They attended Kwantlen University College together, graduated in 1998 and then established and incorporated BYU Design in 2003. Both professional members of the Interior Designer's Institute of British Columbia, Cheryl and Ada have experience that serves as a solid foundation for their relatively young and

LEFT
The private Burnaby residence's living room is both comfortable and elegant
for entertaining.
Photograph by Ed White Photographics

59

highly regarded company. Insistent that documentation is just as important as creative style, BYU Design has been setting itself apart by delivering clearly defined technical documents—even receiving compliments from contractors on the impressive level of detail. For every project, clients are presented with detailed guidelines that take the mystery out of the process, allowing them to clearly understand industry jargon. Beginning on the macro level, BYU Design takes its projects from inception, through space planning, finishing, concept development, all the way to the micro level of detailed accessorizing with plates, napkins and lighting. Although work mainly includes multiunit projects such as condominium towers and townhouse developments, BYU Design also works on a variety of private residential and hospitality design projects.

Cheryl and Ada say it is easy to be inspired in a city such as Vancouver—besides having office views of majestic mountains and rolling oceans, local products and furniture designers offer endless opportunities to excel in their design work. Operating within such a progressive area as Vancouver has also opened many doors creatively; most clients are very accepting of new and unconventional styles. Now that green principles have become the standard, clients have come to ask initial questions not only about colour palettes but also those regarding sustainable processes and finishes. One of the highest priorities of BYU Design is ensuring that clients receive a space where they can function properly, and oftentimes this requires working outside of the designer's personal taste to deliver the best space in the best style.

TOP LEFT
A dramatic foyer features a wooden barrel vault, edgeless glass stair rail and formal dining room.
Photograph by Ed White Photographics

BOTTOM LEFT
Designed in a casual West Coast traditional style, the master bedroom has a neutral palette with vibrant, light-pouring views.
Photograph by Martin Tessler

FACING PAGE
Hardwood floors and built-in storage with buffet complement the elegant dining area.
Photograph by Martin Tessler

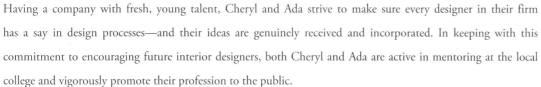

Having a company with fresh, young talent, Cheryl and Ada strive to make sure every designer in their firm has a say in design processes—and their ideas are genuinely received and incorporated. In keeping with this commitment to encouraging future interior designers, both Cheryl and Ada are active in mentoring at the local college and vigorously promote their profession to the public.

Set apart not just by name, but also with its ability to incorporate distinctive human warmth into each project, BYU Design sets a standard for the very bright future of interior design.

ABOVE LEFT
The drama and mood of a modern and inviting dining room is perfect for evening entertainment.
Photograph by Martin Tessler

ABOVE RIGHT
Stainless-steel appliances and accessories, along with surprising hints of colour through accent pieces, make this kitchen a perfect example of modern design within a compact space.
Photograph by John Sinal Photography

FACING PAGE
A built-in bench, storage with platform bed and upholstered headboard combine within the master bedroom to offer a perfect balance of comfort and functionality.
Photograph by Martin Tessler

ROBERT CAPAR

MAISON D'ETRE DESIGN-BUILD INC.

When Robert Capar purchased a dilapidated house in Vancouver's West End he had no idea that it would lead him to realize his dream of developing a design-build firm. The house, originally owned by a prosperous businessman, had been converted into an 11-unit boarding house and stood in a state of complete disrepair. The eventual transformation of this rundown house brought recognition to the skills, design expertise and integrity that have become hallmarks of maison d'etre design-build inc.

Since 1995 maison d'etre has built its reputation on the premise that the design of a house can be both forward-thinking and simultaneously healthy with the use of natural products, fibers and building materials. The firm strives to produce innovative designs that enhance property value and marketability, but perhaps more importantly, to ensure that the house will remain livable and grow with the homeowner's changing needs.

Its signature style is reflected throughout completed projects—functionality, lighting, the use of natural products and finishes and the interconnection of interior and exterior

spaces. By applying current trends and styles, maison d'etre re-envisions and transforms dated designs through the design-build renovation process.

The firm believes that everyone deserves good design—whether the client is building a home to raise a family or entering retirement, maison d'etre is keenly focused on achieving its vision. The opportunity to design and build new homes provides for limitless design options compared to the renovation process, although the costs for either option can be equivalent.

ABOVE
The expansive view from the exterior gives the striking impression of the dining room floating above the living room.
Photograph by Multivista Construction Documentation Inc.

FACING PAGE
Placing the living area on the lower level with a dramatic two-story window creates a dynamic space in this open floorplan home.
Photograph by Multivista Construction Documentation Inc.

If an original structure has redeeming features, renovation is a reasonable option. The concept of renovating also allows for the reduction of materials otherwise destined for landfills and meshes with maison d'etre's green-build philosophy.

The firm's continual commitment to innovative and timeless solutions has been recognized with both National SAM Awards and Provincial Georgie Awards. To give homes a visual presence and functionality and to integrate green building and modern technologies in a cohesive manner—this is the goal of maison d'etre design-build inc.

TOP LEFT
Over-height windows with low sills create a sense of openness with a connection to exterior spaces in this cozy informal gathering room off the kitchen.
Photograph by Multivista Construction Documentation Inc.

BOTTOM LEFT
Vibrant colours and cabinetry define the entry, dining room, family room and kitchen; an outdoor deck and a powder room complete the floorplan.
Photograph by Multivista Construction Documentation Inc.

FACING PAGE
Warm cherry cabinets highlight the kitchen and offset the unifying neutral gray oak flooring, granite and polished concrete floor on the lower level.
Photograph by Multivista Construction Documentation Inc.

RUS COLLINS
DIANNE KENNEDY

ZEBRA DESIGN & INTERIORS GROUP

Dianne Kennedy believes the house is a tool of analysis for the human soul. Her philosophy is paired with colleague and owner of Zebra Design and Interiors Group, Rus Collins, who launches each project with a stripping down of the space to its bare form and function. Only when a home is reborn with accoutrements can it reflect the individual client's lifestyle, personality and specific needs.

At Zebra Design, emphasis is placed on giving rooms a fluency of scale. In order to be successful, a home must be livable before the layers of décor can be applied and finished. Rus begins his creative process in designing each home long before the first colour palette or tile sample are even considered. Intuitively, Rus is able to read his clients' desires and expectations. From the first meeting clients are immediately put at ease. Initial consultations are relaxed and often like a social gathering. But make no mistake—this is where the genius quotient steps in.

Zebra Design believes that the home is a reflection of its occupants and how they live. By allowing people to express their dreams, which are many times quite different, clients are able to participate in the realization of their greatest expectations. At this point, Rus and Dianne become alchemists of design. Truly listening to their clients regarding lifestyle, use of space, family needs and personal preference, they employ their years of experience and natural appreciation of space to develop custom designs that allow the personalities of the owners to flow throughout.

ABOVE
Indigenous, natural materials integrating with clean, strong lines raise the bar on traditional West Coast style. Martha Sturdy's 48-inch spun disc complements the mirror.
Photograph by Vince Klassen

FACING PAGE
The house sits on Chesterman Beach, Tofino. Internationally known for great surfing and wild West Coast storms, Tofino has morphed into one of North America's toniest hideaways.
Photograph by Vince Klassen

There is no design style that Rus is not willing to consider. The streets of Victoria are graced by an abundance of his firm's designs, from the most detailed Arts-and-Crafts home to contemporary pieces. Timelessness, exquisite attention to detail, use of sustainable building materials and pure good taste are the marks of a Zebra Design home. Zebra homes are not restricted to Victoria locations; Rus, Dianne and the Zebra team have designed all over Vancouver Island, North America and as far away as the Bahamas.

Rus works with Dianne from the very beginning of a project to ensure that the architectural and aesthetic elements will thread together seamlessly. Once the architectural bones are established, they collaborate often throughout the entire design process to ensure that all the clients' needs have been considered. Dianne is a tour de force of knowledge regarding art, interior design materials, suppliers and the latest trends on the market. Her abilities to merge the elements of good aesthetics with Rus' innovative architectural design provide their clients with an end result that consistently brings an exceptional level of comfort, satisfaction and pride.

TOP LEFT
An important art collection was paramount to the design process. Walls of slatted fir add dimension to the open plan through materials and shadowing effects.
Photograph by Vince Klassen

BOTTOM LEFT
The clients, admitted oenophiles, were actively involved in the design of the climate-controlled, well-thought-out wine cellar to house their impressive collection.
Photograph by Vince Klassen

FACING PAGE
The kitchen, a gastronomic oasis, provides an outlet for creative "culinary stress release" for the busy clients, a surgeon and an anaesthesiologist.
Photograph by Vince Klassen

MILA DJURAS

INTERMIND DESIGN INC.

Mila Djuras embraces the principle that a house mirrors its occupants and should be a giving, accommodative and interactive habitat for the owner's self. She understands that the house reflects its occupants, and in turn she interprets and comprehends what it is communicating—ultimately acting on what the house is striving to portray. Mila believes that design should be a pure and fluid reflection of the self, creating environments that encourage a holistic interaction of clients' physical, mental, emotional and spiritual well-being.

She innovates—never mass produces—through the design-build process. While Mila has respect for tradition, she is not in favor of repeating or embracing it. Present-day creative contemporaries should filter tradition, re-interpret it, possibly incorporate its timeless or universal values, but always reinvent it so that the final product reflects today's thoughts, values and accomplishments.

Both architecturally and spatially, Mila creates comfortable spaces and makes the design process a smooth and enjoyable journey. By considering the formation of a stairwell, the dimensions of a living room or the manner in which natural light floods through particular windows, Mila facilitates environments for interactive living within the limitations of the space.

Mila often works with artists to enhance a space's interior architecture through colourful, graphical and sculptural elements. Mila believes that an architectural interior or exterior can be neutral, yet not inactive—again, rhythm, texture, colour and symbols should deliver a message. Clients are included in every step of the design process with Intermind Design. Mila's inclusive approach is facilitated by her interest in design and social psychology—there is a will to guide each client into a renewed sense of self.

ABOVE
The pattern created by walnut wood flooring on the top of the stairs and reflective stainless steel on the risers is complemented by natural light from a skylight and a striped mural inspired by Sol LeWitt.
Photograph by Luis Pascual

FACING PAGE
The art display wall inserted unit with stainless-steel background contains ethnic-inspired sculptures, masks and pottery from local, Asian and African artists.
Photograph by Luis Pascual

Her projects have an impressive variety, showcasing an intuitive understanding of what a space and its inhabitants require. For one project, a large-scale children's indoor playhouse, Mila researched child behavior patterns and colour coding that would encourage proper, balanced brain activity during extended play sessions. By having visual transparency throughout the entire space, parents and children had a constant connection to each other.

While she approaches every project with the highest level of professionalism, Mila tries to incorporate a sense of humor when possible. For an exhibition at BC Place called "Ultimate Dog House," she designed an ultimate male garage with a toilet situated on top of a staircase so that sports results can still be viewed from the half-open bathroom. Along with this haute-couture toilet is a shower that uses the same mechanics as a car wash—shampoo and soap automatically dispense from the shower and by pressing another button, water rinses its occupant clean. This project exemplifies Mila's unique customization and fearlessness in devising untraditional solutions.

Mila notes that colours in nature flow, that nothing seems out of place in an environmental setting—there is always a captivating element. This is the same approach she takes with her projects. Whatever the area within a home, there should be multiple activities taking place to provide complexity and variety without being overwhelming.

LEFT
A Thai spirit house and indoor yellow-sand garden are placed on the mezzanine level, separating the stairway and accenting a mid-century Eero Saarinen tea table that is surrounded with traditional black Chinese chairs.
Photograph by Luis Pascual

FACING PAGE
This sitting area is made complete with an elongated white Italian sofa and organic transparent coffee table along with a feminine Dutch Leolux chair. The home library is located one step up next to two-story windows that face Victoria Park.
Photograph by Luis Pascual

One way in which she incorporates an organic approach is to introduce a material—stainless steel, for example— in unexpected ways. Yes, an oven or refrigerator could be expected to have some form of stainless steel, but to provide balance, Mila might incorporate the same material into stairs, dropped ceiling or wall treatment as well.

In a more traditional, full-scale re-build renovation, Mila delivered a home-sanctuary that incorporates high functionality of contemporary design with the client's cultural and spiritual values, emphasizing the diverse ethnicities within Vancouver's growing international population. Mila designed the exterior with post-modernist colours to showcase key features by incorporating two-floor, 18-foot front windows. Inside the home, she opened the floorplan and separated spaces by using platforms, columns, drops, beams and displays. Mila chose glass doors, walnut flooring, countertops and steps made of polished stone along with glass and acrylic furniture in order to provide complete visual transparency indoors and projecting outdoors.

Whether she is working on a house or commercial space, Mila considers the distinct elements that each room needs to embrace so that clients feel physically and psychologically comforted.

RIGHT
Industrial Italian tiles in several patterns are used to create a neutral palette as the contrasting background for the dynamic wall sculpture made by Mila's husband, artist Branko Djuras. The result is a Zen-like ambience with an abstract interpretation of the centrally placed tree.
Photograph by Luis Pascual

FACING PAGE
An open interior plan is created by platforms, ceiling drops, customized built-ins, columns and beams. Visual transparency is confirmed with the repeated use of glass doors and walnut flooring; polished stone on counters and steps; stainless steel on stair risers, appliances, lighting and bathroom fixtures; as well as glass and acrylic furniture and chandeliers.
Photograph by Luis Pascual

DEBBIE EVANS

WHISTLER INTERIOR DESIGN

When her mother came home from work each day to find the living room furniture rearranged for the third time in one week, it was just a small clue that elementary-aged Debbie Evans was already preparing for the world of interior design. And now with more than a decade of experience behind her, Debbie brings Whistler residents not just a home, but a crafted sanctuary built from the work of endless local artisans.

One of the many reasons Debbie enjoys working in Whistler is the varied access to skilled people. When a client is searching for a piece of furniture, Debbie and her team enthusiastically incorporate numerous design elements to produce a piece that is anything but standard. Even the most daunting designs are met with endless brainstorming and interactive planning with local craftsmen. The smallest customizations deliver a well-crafted home every time.

A particular home that stands out in Debbie's mind is one that was placed on a vast deal of land—more than 40 acres to be exact. For the area, where most homes are cantilevered into the side of the mountain, this project proved inspiring for many reasons. Not only could the design team work with a rustic log cabin placed on a timber frame, but for once, they were able to design around the expansive views that the architect had skillfully incorporated.

Upon visiting a home or its future build site, Debbie finds that the architecture speaks to her—revealing what would be the most harmonious path of design. With renovations, the team at Whistler Interior Design tries to follow the lines of the house and improve upon them. While Debbie designs numerous kitchens and bathrooms and enjoys the millwork detailing, she has found over the years that being involved in a house project from the very beginning is highly rewarding. She works with the architect to perfect the layout before anything is built and continues to contribute her expertise during the specification process where furniture and window coverings are chosen. Following a home from the auto-cad detailing all the way to the final placement of a vase of flowers allows the Whistler design team to display its customization proficiency.

ABOVE
The staircase was given great attention and now serves as the focal point from all the rooms, providing a central area that resembles a piece of art.
Photograph by Insight Photography

RIGHT
This steam shower is a perfect natural setting for a spa—it brings the outdoors in with natural stones shaped into mountain peaks and warm terracotta-coloured tile.
Photograph by Insight Photography

FACING PAGE
Divided from the kitchen with an Old World-style arch, the bar looks as if it has grown into the middle of the room—replete with natural elements such as tree-root bases, wood-slab tops and stone.
Photograph by Insight Photography

With local ski resorts, mountains and pristine water, Debbie is inspired by the relaxing nature as well as the varied multitudes of people these elements attract. One of her clients, who was of British descent and lived in Hong Kong, requested Debbie's renovation services for a house he had recently purchased. In the end, the client was both surprised and thrilled with the traditional, British-style house that had splashes of Asian influence mixed throughout; upon completion, he declared it was his favorite home.

Each new project brings Debbie and the design team at Whistler Interior Design the opportunity to transform visions into tangible living spaces, within budget while embracing creativity, one client at a time.

LUCILLE FARES

LMF INTERNATIONAL
INTERIOR DESIGN CONSULTANTS, INC.

Lucille Fares is a maverick. Born in England and raised in Egypt and Asmara, she spent her younger days filtering through the Middle East, Africa and Europe. Her family traveled extensively, ingraining in her a lifelong appreciation for regions and their respective cultures—wherever she went, she absorbed design and detail. Upon entering the professional world of interior design, she established her first office in Dubai and initially worked with an associate in Hong Kong, developing classical Chinese furniture as well as Western concepts. During that time she also undertook interior design projects for expatriate and local clients in the region and in Heidelberg, Germany.

LEFT
Spectacular views of English Bay, Vancouver, are the backdrop that wraps around a downtown beach-side condominium. A palette of pale cream walls, rich exotic woods and cool, crisp upholstery is used to enhance and showcase the clients' eclectic collection of Turkish carpets. The design incorporates modern clean lines with highlights of the Orient from Eurasia to Southeast Asia.
Photograph by Ivan Hunter

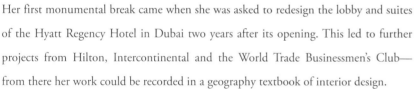

Her first monumental break came when she was asked to redesign the lobby and suites of the Hyatt Regency Hotel in Dubai two years after its opening. This led to further projects from Hilton, Intercontinental and the World Trade Businessmen's Club—from there her work could be recorded in a geography textbook of interior design.

Looking at her projects might reveal traces of the many places Lucille has recorded in her mind's eye: from the classicism of the Roman ruins in Baalbeck and the Egyptian pyramids to the Deco influences of the architecture of cities such as Asmara in Eritrea, Paris, Milan and London. After working in Dubai for more than two decades, she began searching for new influences—a place to broaden her scope and renew her creative energy. In 2004 she opened her interior design firm, LMF International, in Vancouver.

Her extensive work in the Middle East and Europe gave Lucille an opportunity to work with many fabulous antiques as well as modern pieces, but she says that one of the best parts of operating in Vancouver is the challenge to incorporate the panorama and abundance of natural materials into her design. A different, fresh concept is embraced by clients in British Columbia, harmonizing the nature surrounding a home to create internal beauty. Lucille works from the earliest stages on an assortment of projects with diverse people, and her international experience has taught her to adapt and interact with clients even when they don't speak the same language.

Lucille's style leans toward Neoclassicism and is rooted in the belief that all good design stems from the lessons and inspirations of the past and the ability to adapt it to the present. However, she is quick to point out that interior design is not an exact

science—yes she creates sensual and comfortable spaces, but in order to achieve the "wow" factor, inspiration, taste, technical savvy and love must be applied. All the while, she remembers that the most important ingredient is listening to clients and delivering their dreams. Using all of these factors she develops a concept, meticulously pulling inspiration from the elements around her and combining them with the resources within her rich memory bank.

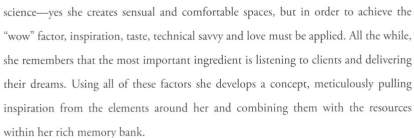

ABOVE LEFT
Artwork by renowned British Columbia-artist Motoko reflects the rich colour palette selected from the jewel and spice tones of the Orient in the use of accessories, seen in rich silks and brocades for the cushions. The palette was cleverly used throughout the apartment to create continuity, but by highlighting different combinations, each room clearly has its own identity.
Photograph by Ivan Hunter

ABOVE RIGHT
The pale-green pama wood veneered wall panel coordinates with the show-stopping 12-inch handmade silver handle from France, creating a stunning piece of art while cleverly concealing the plasma television. The floating desk—constructed of dyed, reconstituted wenge wood—also conceals the entertainment center. The Lucite chair from Philippe Starck adds to the floating impression of these pieces without breaking up the line.
Photograph by Ivan Hunter

FACING PAGE LEFT
Turkish calligraphy; a French antique-inspired black crystal and chrome lamp sitting on a galleried silver tray table; a black and white cowhide ottoman; and a rich Turkish rug combine to create a modern but uniquely oriental style, which showcases the clients' long history of travel.
Photograph by Ivan Hunter

FACING PAGE RIGHT
The architecture of the terrace resembling the prow of an ocean liner draws one out to sea. Continuing this theme, the Moroccan hand-beaten, recycled aluminum table with Arabian lantern is flanked by steel chairs and cushions from Jim Thompson.
Photograph by Ivan Hunter

Ask Lucille if she has a mantra or motto for her firm and she politely replies that she does not. It is her belief that everyone should wake up in the morning with a mind open to the day's possibilities, endeavoring to rise a little higher than the day before. She is not confined by boundaries and preconceptions. The greatest chefs, designers and artists—whom she modestly aspires to join—exude a natural instinct; conformity does not produce liberty.

Continuing in her journey to design spaces of impact that incorporate the serenity and panoramic scope of Vancouver, Lucille is reveling in the perspective of this forward-thinking locale. Her projects continue to be recognized internationally through numerous media markets including CNN and the *Today* show. One of her projects in British Columbia, The Tent House Suites at Rockwater Secret Cove Resort, has been rated among the top 25 in the world of its genre by *Travel + Leisure* magazine. Having spent vast amounts of time in the East and now based in the West, Lucille remains an extensive traveler, and her unique background and experience are highly sought after. Her expanding portfolio is evidence of an innate ability to deliver her clients' visions while remaining true to her artistic conscience.

TOP RIGHT
The antique brass and copper Italian espresso machine highlights the use of bronze and silver ceramic Italian tiles for the backsplash and the rich emperador marble counters.
Photograph by Ivan Hunter

BOTTOM RIGHT
The kitchen is the center of the apartment and has spectacular 180-degree views of the bay. The custom cabinetry is in vertical-grain fir with panels of reconstituted macassar ebony. Tiny, Oriental-inspired Swarovski crystal pendant lights were used in the corridors and the entrance hall, bringing an unexpected soft and feminine touch to the strong notes of the cabinets.
Photograph by Ivan Hunter

FACING PAGE TOP
Drama has been added to the dining room with the antique, red-lacquered Chinese sideboard and dramatic artwork by Motoko. The white, loosely covered chairs add texture without detracting from the drama of the wall, and the embroidered initials of the clients are a very Oriental and rich touch.
Photograph by Ivan Hunter

FACING PAGE BOTTOM
The table settings continue the Oriental theme with Japanese-inspired dishes and delicate chartreuse hydrangeas and orchids with deep red centers.
Photograph by Ivan Hunter

DAMION FARRELL

FĪV DESIGNS

As a young boy Damion Farrell could be found happily tracing the fabric swatches in furniture and fabric stores. He would seemingly disappear among the large sample racks, allowing them to engulf him in their textures and colours. Even to this day, when sourcing for clients Damion enjoys the process of combing through the various visual and tactile options. His fascination with design and the nuances that define them was further bolstered by exposure to many environments he was exposed to as a child. Damion's design foundation was influenced greatly by these experiences, through which he learned that great beauty cannot only be found in a beautifully designed environment but also in simplicity, the old and worn, and even in that which is intrinsically flawed. After a prolific career as a graphic designer, Damion knew that his life's work lacked passion. With a substantial overlap of colour theory and design principles, the transition into the full-time position of an interior designer was every bit delightful and exciting.

As the principal of Fīv Designs (pronounced "five"), Damion has etched a niche for himself in client-centric design. While most homeowners inquire about his personal style, Damion gladly explains that the essence of every space must be influenced by its occupants. After in-depth research into his clients' style and motivation, Damion applies a minimalist approach to any genre that may be sought. This ever-fluid design approach keeps Damion on his toes, allowing him to develop a stronger style that understands his clients' requests.

ABOVE
Louis XV-style furniture with rich woods, silver inlays and soft-coloured damasks adorns this Richmond home.
Photograph by Jamie Drouin

FACING PAGE
Serenity and peacefulness of an ocean scene was the inspiration for this Vancouver townhouse that combines centuries-old antiques with modern minimalism.
Photograph by Jamie Drouin

Further enhancing Damion's portfolio is an eclectic mix of residential designs. Ensuring that each new home stands out from the one before, he stays tuned in to the simple things around him. Inspiration is often found in the colouration of a tree, product packaging or even a bed of flowers—by stepping back and appreciating the object for more than its face-value, Damion translates what he sees and consequently re-invents the traditional and expected elements within a home.

Understanding that this large-project process can often be frustrating—and rarely encouraging to the virtue of patience—Damion instills confidence in his clients that the end result is worth the journey. He is guided by the belief that a home influences the subconscious and alters individual and group interaction, and such an entity can never be rushed. By focusing on the pieces and colours that his clients naturally gravitate toward, Damion produces effective and transformative environments.

TOP LEFT
Polished silvers, soft metallic accents and white leather in the dining area accentuate the reflection of the modernized depiction of Anton Mauve's painting.
Photograph by Jamie Drouin

BOTTOM LEFT
The use of solid maple, sea-green silk and sandstone linen creates a cozy bedroom with the tranquility of the calm, open waters.
Photograph by Jamie Drouin

FACING PAGE
The living area is further adorned with weathered suede textures, contemporary coloured silk damask, pops of crisp blues and modern classics to complete the room.
Photograph by Jamie Drouin

Amanda Forrest

AMANDA FORREST
INTERIOR DESIGN CONSULTING

In today's world of do-it-yourself decorating shows, many people have a subtle message delivered to them: Only clients with extensive budgets can afford the services of a professional design firm. But with Amanda Forrest Interior Design consulting, beauty has a range of price points. Clients who meet with Amanda Forrest find that design services are indeed within reach; the satisfaction of transforming a kitchen, bath or perhaps even a complete living space within a fair budget proves to be very rewarding to Amanda and the client.

From drawings to floorplans and colour schemes, clients appreciate the familiarity that comes from working directly with Amanda upon their initial contact with the firm. While she does have other experienced team members who assist her in implementing her designs, Amanda makes it a priority to oversee all aspects of her projects.

A young couple once enlisted Amanda's services in redesigning and infusing modernistic flavors into a plain and dilapidated house. Applying a present-day aesthetic without causing the home to look out of place was a challenge, but Amanda and her team keenly designed a sophisticated-looking shell, giving the house a thoughtful renovation both inside and out. An uplifting colour scheme was incorporated while maintaining the original architectural elements of the house; modern lighting and contemporary furnishings balanced the older lines of the house, giving a clean look to a space that needed a fresh approach.

Amanda takes this same technique into every new assignment, occasionally finding that certain projects inspire her just as much as the numerous design shows she attends each year. In one specific instance, a client requested an unusual colour palette that inspired Amanda to repaint her entire house. Transitioning from warm to cool colours, she incorporated a more masculine presence by using grays and charcoals while also updating her furnishings and artwork.

Traveling excursions are yet another avenue by which Amanda broadens her design scope. Two trips—one to Hong Kong, another to Australia—left particular impressions that she has tried to incorporate into her designs. The hotel she visited in Hong Kong offered a boutique style that she enjoys weaving into principal suites, while the simplistic Australian beach house offered new ideas on heated concrete floors, flat rooflines and high-gloss kitchens.

It is easy to observe why clients repeatedly return to Amanda for her design services. Often the responses echo the same sentiments: She knows how to interpret her clients' style. Not only do they appreciate the sophisticated and traditional furnishings she selects, but they also love how Amanda imparts a modern glamour that keeps spaces from becoming stale. Simply put, her designs embrace a distinct longevity that continues to set Amanda Forrest Design at the forefront of interior design.

TOP RIGHT
This contemporary kitchen was designed with functionality and family gatherings in mind. The contrasting palette and striking wood floor add visual interest and warmth.
Photograph by Concept Photography

BOTTOM RIGHT
This room within the Musto family's home was completely gutted before being reconceived. Modern lighting and retro-inspired furnishings breathe new life into this space.
Photograph by Concept Photography

FACING PAGE LEFT
An organic colour palette seamlessly blends the coastal waterfront with the Struch family's living room. Soft furnishings and seaside accessories keep the feeling gracious and sophisticated.
Photograph by Concept Photography

FACING PAGE RIGHT
The open entertaining area affords guests the opportunity to dine in style while surrounded by ocean waves crashing the shore.
Photograph by Concept Photography

MITCHELL FREEDLAND

MITCHELL FREEDLAND DESIGN

Mitchell Freedland had a fascination with the intricacies of grand hotel lobbies from a very young age. Mitchell says that interior design has always been within him, instilled by the memories of visiting hotels with his parents.

After earning an honours diploma in environmental design at Ontario College of Art, Mitchell worked with interior designers in Vancouver and New York before establishing his namesake firm in 1993. More than 20 years' experience has allowed his expertise to be applied in a plethora of projects—hotels, restaurants, libraries, airline lounges and more—from Los Angeles to Chicago, at home and as far away as Tokyo, his design fingerprints make a lasting and international impression.

LEFT
The waterfront penthouse condominium infused a warm, neutral palette and a refined tailored
ambience to enhance the ever-changing majesty of the sea and sky beyond.
Photograph by Ed White Photographics

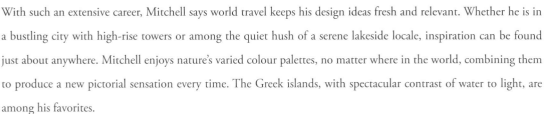

With such an extensive career, Mitchell says world travel keeps his design ideas fresh and relevant. Whether he is in a bustling city with high-rise towers or among the quiet hush of a serene lakeside locale, inspiration can be found just about anywhere. Mitchell enjoys nature's varied colour palettes, no matter where in the world, combining them to produce a new pictorial sensation every time. The Greek islands, with spectacular contrast of water to light, are among his favorites.

It is this connection to nature that has often provided inspiration for his designs. With a recent hotel lobby in Hawaii, he used stained cherry wood to give the impression of teakwood, creating an indigenous feel to the space. The additional juxtaposition of pale limestone, along with the teakwood look, brought a dramatic contrast.

This waterfront duplex penthouse received its colour inspiration from the warmth and glow of the light dancing off the water. Pale neutrals with warm sand and honey colours are the perfect complement to this beachfront location, giving a year-round summer house appeal.

Mitchell Freedland Design operates as a team to cultivate an end result that is not only classic, but extremely tailored, cohesive and pristinely enduring. Mitchell has confidence that his designs—whether a residence, restaurant, hotel lobby or another unique commission—will stand the test of time and deliver striking first impressions to all who experience them.

ABOVE LEFT
The fully customized kitchen has the warmth and continuity of satinwood, used throughout the suite.
Photograph by Ed White Photographics

ABOVE RIGHT
The entry library offers a peaceful retreat within the heart of the penthouse.
Photograph by Ed White Photographics

FACING PAGE
The master suite of the duplex penthouse floats above the bay, incorporating the ethereal palette established by the residence.
Photograph by Ed White Photographics

NINA HAMILTON

NAPANEE DESIGN LTD.

Fabrics, colours and paint charts usually accompany the typical description of any interior designer. But for Nina Hamilton and the design team at Napanee Design, projects involve so much more. While the coordination of details is essential in every endeavor, Napanee Design works as both facilitator and translator—bringing life to its clients' visions by taking intangible ideas and creating practical environments. Working as a translator for her clients is where Nina finds the most joy in her profession.

Creating unpretentious spaces is essential to every Napanee Design project, and Nina says the humanness and informality to the Vancouver environment operates as an inspiration to her designs. Keeping in step with the West Coast's carefree and casual lifestyle, every project is designed to be livable, human and comfortable. Clients must be able to settle and feel at home in their environments, and in order to meet this standard Nina spends a significant amount of time learning their various idiosyncrasies. Their professions, tastes and history form the backdrop for every design, allowing their personality and style to be reflected.

One of the many goals at Napanee Design is that each home must look as if it has evolved over time, without the help of an interior designer. When designing a recent beach house, the Napanee Design team pulled a mix of styles together. Anchoring the living room is a fireplace that is anything but ordinary. To encourage the sense of history to this particular house, special attention was paid to the fireplace by taking it through three generations of history—first by painting the brick and then putting a white wooden painted façade on it. Keeping with the beach house ambience, the bricks were positioned to resemble a slumped sand castle. In order to reinforce the historic feeling of the beach house, an antique bamboo rug and table were added to the entry and master bedroom.

Through each project, Nina strives to follow her company's mantra and create environments that uplift the human spirit. Whether designing a summer retreat by the beach or a cozy log cabin, she aims to make beauty a necessity—while making necessity beautiful.

ABOVE LEFT
Battened and antiqued walls pair up with the historical tradition of the painted hardwood floors in East Coast summer homes, encouraging an endless state of relaxation.
Photograph by Robert Kent

ABOVE RIGHT
Vibrant colours and strong patterns overlay the neutral backdrops of this lively breakfast room. Its carefree nature defines the essence of beach living.
Photograph by Joanne Richardson

FACING PAGE
Evolution of a century or two was condensed into weeks with the development of a layered, whitewashed fireplace. Painted paneling, distressed flooring and antique lighting contribute to the sense of history.
Photograph by Joanne Richardson

JENNIFER HEFFEL
LESLI BALAGNO

HEFFEL BALAGNO DESIGN CONSULTANTS

Achieving a truly custom look requires a tailored approach, a design plan in which every detail nods to the overall idea and a profusion of one-of-a-kind furnishings. But most importantly, such an effect demands the creative and organizational skills of professional interior designers like Jennifer Heffel and Lesli Balagno, who are well-versed in creating the custom look that's right for each client's aesthetic tastes and lifestyle.

Jennifer and Lesli met at the University of Manitoba, determined that their design philosophies were a good match and formed Heffel Balagno Design Consultants in 1995. Their creative process is client-centric and unprecedentedly comprehensive. The designers get involved at the earliest architectural planning stages and see their projects through construction and installation to completion.

Jennifer and Lesli have a knack for reading clients of all ages and from all walks of life. Locals looking for a primary or vacation residence and international patrons who long for that enticing West Coast lifestyle appreciate the designers' sense of style and relaxed approach. Jennifer, Lesli and their team distill the world of interior architectural styles down to the very best options.

Rather than slowly progressing through the home one room, one surface at a time, Jennifer and Lesli initially focus on one or two main spaces and architectural details: the kitchen, master bathroom and fireplace, perhaps. Based on this concentrated group of spaces and details, the designers create a formula for the design, which is carried through the millwork, fixtures and colour palette, and then reinterpret this formula throughout the balance of the interiors. For example, the two-inch stone counter may lead into a standard proportion for the millwork gables; a mosaic backsplash may evolve into a large-scale floor pattern or inspire a custom carpet. This attention to both the big picture and the fine details—and how they relate—ensures a consistent, polished, custom look. As well, the design formula empowers homeowners to make wise decisions that will complement their residence's timeless aesthetic long after the project is complete.

ABOVE LEFT
The spiral staircase creates a strong architectural statement and is anchored by the custom-designed light fixture, which frames its opening.
Photograph by Philip Jarmain

ABOVE RIGHT
Custom-designed furniture accentuates the home's meticulous detailing while Asian sensibilities add to its tranquil nature.
Photograph by Philip Jarmain

FACING PAGE
Inspired by Asian aesthetics, the design for this home was developed through the use of simple massing, clean architectural details and refined beautiful forms.
Photograph by Philip Jarmain

The design package for each project is meticulously laid out in a specification manual that includes every detail relevant to the home's ultimate look. Complete construction drawings along with plumbing, hardware, appliance, lighting and finish specifications provide both the contractor and the client with a clear, concise expectation of the finished project prior to framing. Custom furniture is also an important ingredient in Heffel Balagno's interiors. The style, proportion and colour need to follow the established language of the interiors so as not to jeopardize the design continuity. Jennifer and Lesli have the creative savvy and worldwide industry connections to produce beds, tables, lighting fixtures, hardware, rugs, upholstery and anything else their refined compositions demand.

For their unwavering attention to cohesiveness of style, timelessness, complete customization and designs that provide ease of use, the professionals of Heffel Balagno Design Consultants have been widely recognized in print, through awards and by a growing, referral-based clientele.

LIN HEPPNER

ART + COMMERCE DESIGN INC.

While furniture and material selection may account for a good portion of the interior design process, the most important elements are those that simply can't be sketched into a floorplan. Lin Heppner, principal of Vancouver-based ART + Commerce Design is certainly capable of envisioning and executing designs in a precise length of time but she much prefers to create environments and then allow the finishing touches to work themselves into the composition over the course of a few months or even years. She doesn't underestimate the power of the perfect piece, and when it comes to accents and accessories, she wants at least a few of them to directly reflect the interests, travels and even life pursuits of residents—Lin views accent pieces as opportunities to give context to people's lives. While some strive for instant gratification, Lin's clients appreciate her thoughtful approach, allowing their spaces to evolve and proving just how enjoyable she makes the whole process.

Lin's approach to design begins with listening. While she might bring along a few texture or colour samples as catalysts for conversation to the first few meetings, Lin is foremost concerned with figuring out how her clients' lives work so that she can give them the right type of interior—large, open areas for entertaining, private family rooms or a delicate balance of the two. Once she has uncovered her clients' programmatic needs, she can turn her attention to developing the aesthetics, which is the part of interior design that drew her to the profession some time ago. Each project takes on the personality of the client, but all of Lin's work is defined by her well-edited, clean, intelligent style. Lin describes her process as "building up to a very pared down," meaning that she opens her mind—and her clients' minds—to a world of possibilities, chooses the very best and then distills the essence of it all to a refined composition with a contemporary bent. She takes great care to ensure that the basics are timelessly beautiful and then enlivens the space with little twists of the unexpected.

ABOVE
The master bedroom with its neutral, textured colour scheme is a serene and airy oasis with a dramatic city view.
Photograph by Roger Brooks

FACING PAGE
A textured upholstered banquette and adjacent balcony seating offer a comfortable place to enjoy the spectacular ocean and mountain views.
Photograph by Roger Brooks

With a lifelong interest in the liberal arts, a career as an interior designer and an intrinsic fascination with cultures of all sorts, Lin is well positioned for constant design inspiration. She considers herself a modernist but appreciates the beauty and intrigue of cultures and often incorporates an element or idea from another land into her designs—handcarved artifacts from Africa and Asia seem to have universal appeal. Lin has a way of elevating found objects into fine art status: She once happened upon a fascinating-looking four-foot-tall broken fragment from a rug-washing factory in Indonesia, knew she had to have it and promptly installed the piece in her home. Whether she's working on her own home, updating a client's or embarking on a design adventure with a new patron, Lin is always cognizant that her job—meeting interesting people, exploring new aesthetics and enhancing people's lives—is an enviable one and her passion for it is evident in every detail of every interior.

TOP LEFT
The woodburning fireplace in the bar warms up the gleaming walnut floors while the dark walnut bar cabinet doubles as wood storage.
Photograph by Roger Brooks

BOTTOM LEFT
The simple and classic living room furniture is focused on the fireplace; the adjacent open concept dining room is enhanced by dramatic views.
Photograph by Roger Brooks

FACING PAGE
A neutral palette facilitates the open concept of this penthouse apartment; the dining light fixture gives some sparkle as an unexpected organic element.
Photograph by Roger Brooks

LORRAINE KLIMEK

KLIMEK INTERIORS

For Lorraine Klimek, design doesn't revolve solely around the creation of aesthetic interiors. It's about creating a space that resonates with her clients—a haven that changes their whole perception. Since 1998 when she founded her firm, Klimek Interiors, Lorraine has melded her background in business management and design education to create well-appointed, serene residences.

Lorraine's clientele is extensive yet she finds a common denominator among many who commission her. They want a place of retreat. After a long, hectic day her clients want to open their front door and have a peaceful sense of being home. To accommodate this, Lorraine predominantly uses subdued colour palettes of pale to deep neutrals. This technique has a two-fold benefit: A home can serve multiple purposes if appointed properly—restful areas are soothing and unexpected shots of colour add vibrancy and excitement to the active areas.

LEFT
Sepia glazed walls, pale oil-finished wood floors and a mid-tone neutral for the sofa and area carpets create a timeless base. Excitement is accomplished through art and accessories.
Photograph by Ema Peter Photography

By choosing neutral palettes and a diverse and harmonious mixture of woods, Lorraine ensures that her designs easily adapt to new trends, allowing the core of the space to remain steady and facilitating the incorporation of new, high-contrast pieces as designs shift over the years. Within residences, Lorraine avoids furnishings or themes that are overly matched, as they can make a space look contrived and uninspired. She especially likes the dynamic tension that can be created when natural materials such as wood and stone are mixed with manmade materials like Lucite and concrete.

Helping her clients maintain their budget parameters, Lorraine also guides them to spend the significant dollars where it really counts, and mix with well-chosen, less expensive pieces that blend well; she explains that luxurious spaces don't necessarily have to be accompanied by high price tags.

Lorraine and her Klimek Interiors team have extensive experience giving small spaces the same level of luxury as their larger counterparts, which has proven invaluable given Vancouver's history of leading the way in condominium living. Many of the area's units are now in need of renovation, and Klimek Interiors is poised to take on even the most challenging of commissions and design every detail, from space layouts to the smallest decorative accents.

TOP RIGHT
Sepia glazed walls continue through to the master bedroom for continuity. Neutrals are more muted, as is the artwork, to encourage a feeling of serenity.
Photograph by Ema Peter Photography

BOTTOM RIGHT
A sleek and sophisticated kitchen remains bright and open with a clever use of lighting, space and cabinetry.
Photograph by Ema Peter Photography

FACING PAGE LEFT
Drama is created by the red lacquer dining table reflecting the colour in the artwork of the adjacent living area.
Photograph by Ema Peter Photography

FACING PAGE RIGHT
The guest bedroom-cum-office incorporates a sleek sofa bed with custom-sized bedding and eye-pleasing art.
Photograph by Ema Peter Photography

ROBERT LEDINGHAM

LEDINGHAM DESIGN CONSULTANTS

Ledingham Design Consultants is a professional interior design firm offering complete design services to a residential, hospitality and corporate clientele. Led by the principle that good design should project individual style while expressing function and comfort, Robert Ledingham has combined knowledge and experience with extensive sample and reference libraries to give clients exceptional solutions to every design project.

Each project begins with the understanding that excellence is the mandate—an inherent philosophy shared with the firm's clientele. Good design consists of the essential structure of a room, which must not be concealed by arbitrary or superfluous decoration.

Ledingham Design Consultants derives inspiration for designs from the natural charm of the surroundings—the glory of nature: water, trees, mountains, flora and fauna. This indoor-outdoor relationship is an important aspect of the design team's philosophy.

Success depends on the trust one earns by creating good design. Clients rely on the designer's expertise and the manner in which the designer works with skilled trades to create successful projects. Excellence is Leadingham Design Consultants' mandate and it is reflected in every aspect of the organization.

Thirty years of successful service to residential, hospitality and commercial clients has earned the firm's designers both local and international recognition from peers.

ABOVE LEFT
The entry features Makore wood paneling with an emperador marble floor that extends into the powder room. Polished plaster walls form the background for the wood vanity and crystal sink.
Photograph by Ed White Photographics

ABOVE RIGHT
The media room features upholstered wall panels that conceal the surround sound and built-in Makore desk that overlooks the city.
Photograph by Ed White Photographics

FACING PAGE
An antique French Deco dining table and Murano chandelier play against the Andy Warhol art. A silk wall covering and a wool and silk area carpet create a subtle backdrop.
Photograph by Ed White Photographics

ERIC LEE

VICTORERIC DESIGN GROUP

W hen they were left with an unfinished house, thanks to a contractor who disappeared with their financial down payments, Eric Lee and his family decided to dive into the world of home construction. Having already taken a few courses in high school and completed a few class projects, Eric decided at age 18 to develop the design and elevations for his family's home. The fairly simple plan incorporated a raised dining room, a wraparound balcony and an open stairwell. When Eric completed the drawings, his family took them to a draftsperson in order to advance through permit stages. While the design might have seemed amateur to a fully trained designer, it was quite an accomplishment for this budding student and foreshadowed the successful design path to come.

LEFT
A white high-gloss wall shelf defines the living room without confining it. The built-in, flueless EcoSmart™ firebox provides maximum transparency, while the open glass stair treads are set into a linear black stringer and serve as the dominant accent.
Photograph by Eric Lee

Eric credits his education and insightful viewpoints with an invaluable amount of hands-on design experience. He would access job sites to see what blueprints he could find and study the framing and construction details that were visibly available. From there, he learned industry standards and notations, and after graduating from high school he formalized his education with an architecture diploma from BCIT. Shortly after 1997 he founded his firm VictorEric Design Group. His earlier years were spent apprenticing with BOTI and HKG, where he developed his interior design skills.

Over the years, VictorEric Design Group has built its reputation as a multifaceted firm that works with both the exterior and interior design of residential and commercial projects. Extensive interaction with on-site tradespersons has made Eric familiar with

technical details and has provided him the experience to effectively and cohesively envision an entire project. When he produces a set of plans, he considers the trades who will receive them. He pours a significant amount of time into the finer aspects and details, infusing function and purpose into every corner of the space.

In a recent project, Eric reflected these space-saving techniques within his own home, trading traditional walls for partitions—a center island bookcase and media unit that divides the stairs with the living room. Because the space was fairly small, he utilized open glass treads to provide continuity and the illusion of a grander scale. He does not favor one design genre over another; he appreciates and studies them all to find the design elements that he likes. His affinity for the old and the new is evident in his personal home's design—the exterior is reminiscent of a heritage Craftsman home with its steep roof pitch and top floor dormers, but the interior is quite modern with clean, minimal lines.

When Eric sits down to design a client's project, oftentimes he envisions himself within that space in order to effectively develop a comprehensive space plan. In his designs, he ensures that every detail serves a purpose and appropriately delivers an element of timelessness.

TOP RIGHT
White high-gloss millwork is set flush with the kitchen back wall for maximum storage without taking up visual space. The rest of the kitchen incorporates dark-stained wood cabinets with white Caesarstone countertops.
Photograph by Eric Lee

BOTTOM RIGHT
The freestanding bathtub is reflected in this wall of mirrored cabinets over the ensuite vanity counter. Semi-recessed overhanging sinks and mirrors help to enlarge the space.
Photograph by Eric Lee

FACING PAGE LEFT
The exterior has a Craftsman-revival architecture to complement the surrounding homes. This traditional exterior serves as a dramatic, yet pleasant contrast to the clean and contemporary interior.
Photograph by Eric Lee

FACING PAGE RIGHT
The bottom flight of stairs is kept simple with black solid oak treads contrasted by white risers and highlighted with in-wall step lights. The top flight of stairs uses open glass treads to help filter natural light down to the bottom floor.
Photograph by Eric Lee

Eric travels internationally and studies design everywhere he goes, but also finds that his curiosity is sparked when he is simply exploring his hometown restaurants, hotels and boutiques. A self-professed workaholic, he gladly spends a significant amount of time on his designs because he truly enjoys engaging in the various planning stages. The simple reason for his passion: With every project, he gets to dream up that special space, see it come to life and then begin to dream all over again.

His work is as rewarding to him as a finished art piece is to an artist. His devotion to great design is continually recognized through various awards—in 2007 he earned a Gold Georgie award for Best Design for a Renovation. After more than a decade of experience in designing custom homes, VictorEric Design Group continues to produce functional and foreword-thinking spaces.

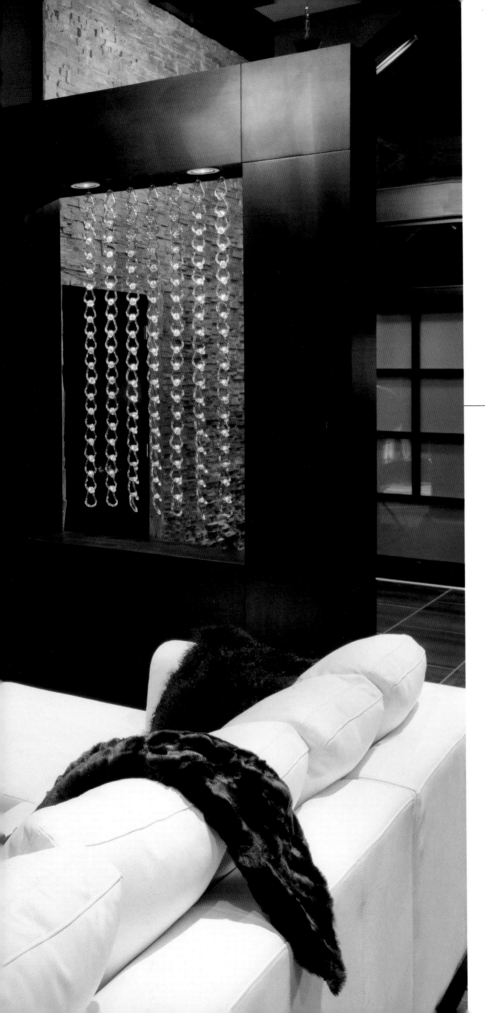

LANA MACRAE

INTERIOR DESIGN GROUP

Good design is forever. And when homeowners have the principal designer, a CAD specialist, a window and fabric specialist and two additional interior designers collaborating on a project, the end result is every bit beyond remarkable. Lana MacRae founded Interior Design Group in 1994 to offer clients a wide array of design options. From turnkey services to small, individualized projects, clients come back repeatedly for the firm's refreshing approach to design.

What mainly drives the style of a home with Interior Design Group is its surroundings and the homeowner's lifestyle—often natural palettes work best with a successful indoor-outdoor relationship. A project can exude simplicity in both modern and traditional designs, but the most important factor is the sense the owners feel when they enter; if their new living space is inspiring and creative, their lives will be impacted positively.

LEFT
Chic, high-styled and sophisticated design unfolds upon entering the home. A ledge stone wall at the entry with a millwork structure featuring inset lighting and glass chainlink showcases an Italian iridescent tile fireplace.
Photograph by Alec Watson

A successful design experience begins with the first contact between designer and homeowner. When both parties come together with ideas—magazine clips, photographs and the like—the home's design can be directed easily through the firm's resource center, ensuring a look that's unique and memorable. Homeowners are drawn to the firm's commitment to aesthetic and functional excellence; the firm exceeds their creative vision while also saving clients time and money by identifying problem areas in both construction and design. With the clients' daily lives and best interests at the forefront of each decision, Interior Design Group gladly collaborates with contractors, suppliers and architects to ensure a project is perfect.

Homeowners work in direct contact with the principal designer, benefiting from supportive interior designers whose additional knowledge brings a chic sophistication and balance within colour, form, texture and light. Artistic renderings, colour boards and CAD drawings give a unique chance for clients to engage with the designers' ideas every step of the way. Never missing a beat in the fundamentals and practice of good design, Interior Design Group adds final touches including pure and luxurious embellishments that are tangible in the custom draperies, bed linens, room accents and more.

Whether Lana and her team are working on a commercial building or a new residence, they approach the project with a fanatical drive. Their work over the past decade has distinguished them as a group that can take a seemingly simple idea and make it extraordinary.

ABOVE LEFT
The exotic veneer kitchen cabinetry grounds the home with a contemporary feel yet adds warmth to the black and white colour scheme throughout the great room. Added into this sleek minimalistic space, the black baroque chandelier mixes it up, creating a hip, modern space. The diamond-shaped windows flank ceiling-to-floor silk draperies in shimmering pewter.
Photograph by Alec Watson

ABOVE CENTER
The home was transformed into a gallery where the furnishings, millwork, finishes and ceiling details take on reoccurring shapes throughout. The simple black and white combination embellished with jewel studded trim adds to the drama and tactile experience.
Photograph by Alec Watson

ABOVE RIGHT
Detailed geometrical shapes draw the eye upward and give personality to each space. The dining room is clean and simple yet adds just the right touch of luxury with velvet draperies and a dazzling crystal chandelier. The circle and square ceiling detail is displayed throughout the home in furnishings as well.
Photograph by Alec Watson

JULIE MAI

JULIE CURTIS DESIGN, INC.

Upon entering the office of Julie Curtis Design, it is impossible for clients not to notice a striking quote: "Quality is never an accident; it is always the result of high intention, sincere effort, intelligent direction and skillful execution." This William Foster sentiment, painted boldly across a 15-foot office wall at Julie Curtis Design, serves as a mantra for Julie Mai and her design team. They recognize that interior design is not something that simply falls out of one's sleeve—transporting a visual aesthetic into a physical reality takes a commitment to excellence that Julie exemplifies.

While her career first began as a faux painter, Julie soon discovered a passion for interior design and the intricacies of an often-complicated process. It was a natural progression from faux finishing into the world of interior design and when Julie completed her education at interior design school, she began working on residential projects. No matter the specified budget, Julie adheres to the belief that a beautiful and functional home should encourage a spirit of renewal for its occupants.

Concerning design specifically, Julie appreciates elegant designs that are well thought out but do not add unnecessary clutter to a space. As D. Ballast wrote, "design requires efficiency, simplicity and elegance with a form consistent with its function." Knowing her clients will have a space that makes their minds feel clear and secure is Julie's greatest reward.

Because the elements of a house should serve a purpose, an integral part of her projects is ensuring that the architecture of the base building feels authentic. When a house's functionality and flow are interrupted, Julie never compromises design by merely camouflaging an area with more clutter—she addresses the problem directly. In the long run, even if a solution requires extensive work, Julie's clients feel confident in such alterations because they trust that her creativity and commitment to authenticity will yield a beautiful haven that puts them completely at ease.

With her clients, Julie's first priority is to make sure that their homes are never a showpiece of her work. By being sensitive to clients' history and endeavoring to incorporate their personal decorative pieces into the new spaces, Julie delivers homes whose designs are highly original but carry the air of effortless elegance.

ABOVE LEFT
The kitchen platform serves three functions: defines the space in an open floorplan, offers an entertaining "stage" and provides better sightlines to the garden.
Photograph by Robert Kent Photo

ABOVE RIGHT
In order to create a bright space for this 1960s' ranch-style house, an open floorplan, ceilings and connection to the outdoors were incorporated.
Photograph by Robert Kent Photo

FACING PAGE
This luxurious, pure and graceful space enhances the bathing experience in the master ensuite.
Photograph by Roger Brooks Photography

VICTORIA McKENNEY

ENVIABLE DESIGNS

After graduating from the University of British Columbia with a degree in art history, Victoria McKenney took a life-changing trip to Europe. As she walked the streets of London, Rome, Monaco and everywhere in between, her art textbooks came to life. Amongst the paintings and sculptures in the British Museum, Uffizi and Louvre, Victoria was inspired to begin an unforeseen but natural progression into the world of interior design. Upon returning to Canada, she made an impressive, energized entry into design, steeped with fresh European influence.

While many young designers spend several years working within various design firms, Victoria's momentum into interior design led her to start her own business, Enviable Designs, at the age of 25. An ever-changing display suite in a Vancouver retail space currently creates a snapshot of her style, allowing prospective clientele to not only see pictures of her work, but to get a sense of Victoria's proficiency in designing with comfortable sophistication. Working with high-profile clients within affluent neighborhoods gives Victoria numerous opportunities to expand design ideas—from contemporary to Mediterranean, she cultivates a distinctive spirit within each project.

ABOVE
Classic coffered ceilings are juxtaposed against a modern faux-lizard wall treatment. The espresso-stained French doors and imported silk draperies suggest a sense of restrained elegance.
Photograph by Brad Anthony

FACING PAGE
In a modern take on Old World charm, this open entrance is accented by a hand-forged wrought-iron railing and antique Biedermeier chair against warm wall tones.
Photograph by Brad Anthony

Commissions vary from simple residential projects to complete top to bottom renovations; yet throughout each space Victoria weaves an element of timelessness. By using classic styles, simple lines and quality materials with a hint of the unexpected, she avoids trendy elements because, above all else, her designs should have a distinct longevity. When Victoria meets with clients, she also shares her fundamental design philosophy: Design is not successful if it is not functional; and with that in mind a strong sense of cohesion must translate into every new project. Barriers to the functionality of a space are addressed so that the appearance of every room harmonizes with the daily lives of the client. From the design concept through problem solving to the final result, Victoria takes great joy in seeing unique designs completed for all her clients.

Today, Victoria breathes new life into her designs by continuing to extensively travel. Each new destination broadens her design concepts—which are instinctively European in both approach and flavor—and provides a path for Victoria to consistently meet the stylistic needs of the eclectic clientele she so fervently serves.

ABOVE LEFT
This definition of indulgence includes opulent handpainted Italian tiles, over-sized Italian marble floor pieces and matching custom vanities capped with Spanish crema marfil limestone.
Photograph by Brad Anthony

ABOVE RIGHT
Tailored layers of rich Bordeaux and soft ivory blend gracefully in the master bedroom. An antique mahogany dress form displays pieces from a client's collection of traditional ethnic clothing.
Photograph by Brad Anthony

FACING PAGE TOP
The travertine wall and floating fireplace add a natural focal point, while the folding glass attracts magnificent views and ocean breezes in true Mediterranean-inspired joie de vivre.
Photograph by Brad Anthony

FACING PAGE BOTTOM
A hand-dyed Persian rug and classically styled furniture are brought together in this living room by antique brass accents and lithographs from local artists.
Photograph by Brad Anthony

FAROUK AND FARIDA NOORMOHAMED

FNDA ARCHITECTURE INC

After more than two decades, FNDA Architecture's portfolio continues to boast a varied and impressive showcasing of residential design. The firm is also well versed in institutional, educational and cultural community development projects. Providing full architectural services, pre-development project analysis and interior design, the firm has a strong and unique foundation upon which its clients can construct state-of-the-art and forward-thinking homes.

With experience in both public and private sector architecture, the firm is grounded in the idea that successful design must be matched with successful project delivery—this can be achieved through a collaborative design process. These innovative design solutions are procured through close communication and established, trusting relationships between clients, consultants and contractors. Time and again, not only are clients' budgets and needs satisfied, but their expectations are exceeded.

A committed pursuit for design excellence results in projects that are recognized for their unique aesthetics, while reflecting the firm's innate ability to harmonize with existing buildings and the natural environment. When clients engage FNDA for residential design, they find that their requests are quite easily met—custom crafted millwork, furnishings, artwork and award-winning lighting design all contribute to the creation of high-quality, distinctive and humane interior spaces. The firm's interior designers utilize their unmatched aesthetic sensibilities with an attention to detail, resulting in a residence that adds to the overall architectural qualities.

ABOVE
Natural lighting filters through the trellis, while the various textures create a spectacular play of light, shadow and colour.
Photograph by Raef Grohne

FACING PAGE
Within the entry court, a tranquil waterfall and courtyard screen the house from the busy street.
Photograph by Raef Grohne

Upon receiving a slew of awards—including international recognition for work on hospitality and residential design—FNDA Architecture stands out as a recognized and respected Vancouver firm. Whether working on a hotel, a Vancouver residence or a religious-based cultural center, the firm remains sensitive to local contexts, traditions and functionality.

TOP LEFT
The entrance hall's art wall, sculptures and sweeping stair give a strong sense of arrival and elegance.
Photograph by Raef Grohne

BOTTOM LEFT
The custom-designed coffee table and Tibetan rug with long sofas create a strong balance and elegance to the conversation area, while also facilitating breathtaking views of Vancouver.
Photograph by Raef Grohne

FACING PAGE LEFT
The original post-and-beam house is reborn by creating a large open space where the structure is celebrated with wood slats and lit custom millwork displays.
Photograph by Raef Grohne

FACING PAGE TOP RIGHT
The babbling fountains, the ledge stone and the fir entrance door root the house into the West Vancouver landscape.
Photograph by Raef Grohne

FACING PAGE BOTTOM RIGHT
The floating hearth and the lightly sandblasted concrete mantel contrast with the slate ledge stone at the fireplace.
Photograph by Raef Grohne

SANDY NYGAARD

NYGAARD INTERIOR DESIGN

Known as a contemporary and modern designer, Sandy Nygaard, principal of Nygaard Interior Design, approaches design with the West Coast's environmental sensibilities in mind.

Interested in materiality, she enlivens a room with the use of wood, stone and fabrics, maximizing their respective textures and colours. Insisting on letting the materials speak for themselves, she uses simple lines and natural colours along with natural light to echo her less-is-more approach.

With each project she approaches, Sandy is passionate about the experiential end result. Guided by the intended use of the space, creative thematic elements are integrated to best express the language needed to define its use. Whether it's a contemporary Tuscan-influenced home or an Asian-fusion restaurant, the greatest satisfaction for Sandy is combining natural materials to create tangible, intelligent spaces.

LEFT
A concrete fireplace paired with surrounding modern furniture offers spacious entertaining.
Photograph by Gary McKinstry

Consistently pushing herself to travel beyond formulaic procedures, Sandy is guided by space, dimension and texture, drawing from both regional and global influences. She enjoys the intricate processes involved with connecting to and interpreting a client's needs. She also stretches her creativity in commercial projects throughout the region including retail, restaurants, resorts and spas where the scale and intended drama is far greater than the expected subtlety in a residence. With an eye for innovation, Sandy weaves together elements that are true to their natural surroundings.

After more than 15 years in the industry she continues to derive energy and excitement from the cohesive design process, creating lasting design and unique living and working spaces.

TOP LEFT
The great room can be seen from second-floor spaces, giving the residence a unique continuity.
Photograph by Gary McKinstry

BOTTOM LEFT
Rich colours and dramatic custom-made light fixtures by Loris Nygaard complete the master bedroom.
Photograph by Gary McKinstry

FACING PAGE TOP
The dining room is generous in size and handsomely accented with commissioned concrete art work by Billie Bjornert.
Photograph by Gary McKinstry

FACING PAGE BOTTOM
Limestone floors, stainless-steel appliances and concrete backsplash are complemented by dark wood cabinets in the kitchen.
Photograph by Gary McKinstry

ELA REZMER

ELA REZMER DESIGN STUDIO

Eager to find a fresh avenue of personal expression, Ela Rezmer was inspired to transition into life as an interior designer when her husband started a real estate investment company in 1997. Leading up to that point, Ela's experiences and travels had led her both personally and professionally through an interest in psychology and the study and eventual practice in dentistry. Through these varied outlets, though, the foundation for Ela's life remained consistent: She wanted to improve people's lives and guide them toward newfound joy, meaning and purpose. The benefits her friends, family and clientele reap are her deepest reward. To support her interior design endeavors, Ela has paired this passion for life with an extensive education, including studies at renowned North American public and private design schools and a master's degree in interior architecture at the Faculty of Architecture & Industrial Design of Academy of Fine Arts in Gdansk, Poland. In addition, Ela continues to enhance her professional education through specialty courses like those she took in Milan, Italy, called "designing designers."

Searching through her recent projects, prospective clients can easily perceive the love Ela pours into her interiors. Influenced by European design, Ela's natural style is simple and elegant, and delicately balances contemporary architectural features with antiques—all the while infusing every space with a discernable timelessness. Her design is intended to serve her clients' needs on every level including mind, body and spirit. Working with this unique and personal approach is the foundation of her design philosophy: Live in the moment. By placing faith in current circumstances—whether good or bad—Ela believes that solutions confidently arise and deliver the best outcome through the design process.

Further illustrating her dedication to artistic expansion, Ela enjoys creating playful and engaging projects. Recently, she designed a bench for the REST public-seating design competition. Aimed at presenting concepts for meaningful, innovative seating for the 2010 Olympic Winter Games, the contest encouraged participants to design with relevant cultural significances. When Ela enlisted the help of her children, David and Daniel, they designed a bench that mimics two people with open arms.

ABOVE
Clean and modern lines are featured in this kitchen, while chocolate tones are complemented by a glass countertop and backsplash. Hidden appliances contribute to the space's streamlined appearance.
Photograph by Spinnermax Inc.

FACING PAGE
The apartment's open design takes advantage of downtown city views.
Photograph by Scott Powell

With two movable heads and three rotating seats—including native motifs and quotes on the back rest—the bench welcomes visitors and encourages the power of play and friendship.

Ela Rezmer Design Studio is a company that is based on integrity, professional ethics, quality of life, innovative solutions and a respect for nature's abundance by a sustainable approach to living by design. Ela's skills mediate between many aspects that influence design, drawing from an extensive knowledge of interior architecture along with industrial, multifamily and residential design. Together, these experiences establish a common ground of understanding for her clients' needs and desires, and use an ever-growing knowledge and experience to design memorable structures. And if ever in need of an idea to springboard into her next project, Ela draws inspiration from nature's intricacies, all forms of artwork—including her newfound passion for sculpting—and a select handful of renowned designers. In fact, Rem Koolhaas' Prada boutique in New York directly inspired a glass gallery she designed in Europe.

Ela—whose life and firm are rooted in Vancouver—happily claims that she lives in the most beautiful area of the country. In such a region, she is given the opportunity to integrate spectacular nature with diverse cultures and translate them into inspiring living spaces. With all this and more greeting her at the beginning of each new day, Ela says that as a designer, she couldn't ask for more.

TOP RIGHT
A striking hood fan, glass bar and cable lighting create an inviting and sophisticated look. The island is designed to facilitate entertaining guests and cooking simultaneously.
Photograph by Ivan Hunter

BOTTOM RIGHT
This thoughtful layout creates a variety of sitting options including an inviting breakfast bar, a casual dining area and an elegant tea corner.
Photograph by Ivan Hunter

FACING PAGE
Modern art creates a backdrop for the casual dining table made of solid maple that can accommodate up to 10 people.
Photograph by Ivan Hunter

VIRGINIA RICHARDS

VIRGINIA A. RICHARDS & ASSOCIATES LTD

Setting the scene for a night of laughter and thoughtful conversation, Virginia Richards' parents would polish silver, arrange the crystal and create fragrant bouquets from the family garden. Their home was a haven for collected treasures that transformed a simple space into one of grace and endless invitation. Her family life certainly well positioned Virginia—known to her friends as Ginny—to understand the art and talent that successful home entertainment demands. Undoubtedly, she also acquired her mother's eye for antiques and her father's persistence in restoring and maintaining these rare items. But rather than embarking on a life of interior design, Ginny felt she had to choose from three typical careers—nurse, teacher or secretary—available to "nice" New Zealand girls at the time. Being the social and inquisitive person that she is, Ginny chose nursing because of the unspoken promise of an overseas job.

Three years after graduating from nursing school, she embarked on her life's dream to travel the world and live in the United States. She journeyed by ship to New York, where she worked in a large hospital, and a year later she settled in Boston for a few years. During this time, she met her Vancouver-born eye-doctor husband—together they decided that Ginny should turn her passion into a business, and thus she dove into her interior design studies.

ABOVE
To reduce exterior city noise, this cozy study has upholstered walls—surrounding family photos, books and personal treasures provide a calm oasis.
Photograph courtesy of Virginia A. Richards & Associates

FACING PAGE
Natural light from a skylight causes the French blue walls to glow in this downtown Vancouver apartment. An 18th-century repousse mirror rests above the desk and beside it rests blooming dogwood in an antique Chinese porcelain vase. The colourful ceramic umbrella stand was imported from Deruta, Tuscany.
Photograph courtesy of Virginia A. Richards & Associates

More than 30 years after founding her firm, Virginia A. Richards & Associates, traces of Ginny's continued explorations emerge in the interiors she designs. With thanks to the influential, uncluttered and appropriately informal style of New Zealand and Australia, Ginny's homes are comfortable, ageless and tailored—an open newspaper won't destroy the look of her designs. With a nod to her upbringing, Ginny's interiors are filled with colour and comfortable furnishings, but she always insists that a home's surroundings should never get in the way of relaxed living. Ever-fascinated by the science of housekeeping, Ginny has an expansive design expertise that carries past the final touches of a home. She goes the extra mile to educate her clients on proper long-term maintenance of their new furnishings.

To this day Ginny still trails across the globe—Paris, London, South Africa and more—to rejuvenate her design focus. The English have taught her the art of harmonizing unmatched items. The French and Italians demonstrate how to live the good life in comfort. Where her life will take her next is unknown, but one thing is certain: Interior design will follow Ginny wherever she goes.

A painted and glazed Sheraton-style wheelback chair is covered in Colefax & Fowler and sits beneath an early oil painting by
Photograph courtesy of Virginia A. Richard.

AB
This room is a sensual balance of luxury enveloping comfort and blends well wit

Photograph courtesy of Virginia A. Richard.

A
An English-inspired bedroom contains upholstered walls, a trimmed canopy and
made of
Photograph courtesy of Virginia A. Richard.

TERESA D. RYBACK

*td*SWANSBURG DESIGN STUDIO

Leonardo da Vinci said that "simplicity is the ultimate sophistication," and this ideal resonates in the work of Teresa Ryback, the principal designer and founder of *td*Swansburg design studio. Her commitment to subtle simplicity and quality design continues to capture the attention of clients both locally and abroad. Her firm has been creating intelligent design solutions since its inception in 2000, earning multiple awards for design excellence. Teresa has distinguished her firm in the design discipline and developed a steady, successful rhythm by undertaking projects that inspire her and her team. This standard, along with ethical guiding principles, leads to designs that whisper timeless elegance and understated luxury.

Specializing in residential and hospitality design, *td*Swansburg began developing interiors that appear effortless, yet have an elusive combination of both form and function. With the belief that interior design and decoration should elevate the architecture of the residence, Teresa begins every project by identifying the historical architectural influences and guides her savvy clients through an informative history lesson. She encourages clients to collect inspirational photos, and then she seamlessly integrates the client's vision of home and individual style while maintaining architectural integrity. As an example of her design firm's flexibility, Teresa approached a contemporary West Coast home and skillfully unified the breathtaking ocean views with her affinity for mid-century modern furniture, and produced a space that has lasting appeal, original personality and simple, classic beauty.

Inspired by the majestic Pacific Northwest surroundings, the striking environments and natural elements often motivate clients to desire more conscientious choices for their projects. Ever concerned with Earth's fragile status, *td*Swansburg continues to forge relationships with eco-friendly suppliers and specify sustainable materials. Whenever possible, the designers locally source expert craftspeople and search for original artwork while managing the details that are vital to a project's success. By maintaining a library of international suppliers, the designers have access to today's leading trends, and clients have a plethora of pertinent options from which to choose.

Having earned her associate's degree in arts and science, Teresa went on to formally study interior design, paralleling her studies with her pursuit to explore the world's leading art galleries and museums. Her passion and dedication for design and architecture—with an artist's eye—allows her to visualize a space in terms of composition, light, colour and texture. Looking toward the future, Teresa and her team at *td*Swansburg design studio see limitless avenues for creative expression in such a thoroughly diverse region. By perpetuating a strong design philosophy and tapping into a myriad of local resources, the future of design is harmoniously synchronizing with the inspired vision of this award-winning West Coast artisan.

TOP RIGHT
The beauty is in the mix. Expansive West Coast ocean views set the backdrop for the designer's love of classic mid-century modern furniture. A Herman Miller Noguchi table and a Le Corbusier chaise lounge share the room with a sleek Century Signature sofa.
Photograph by Alec Watson

BOTTOM RIGHT
A glittering trio of crystal chandeliers, a faux-finished ceiling and opulent damask draperies adorn the dining room. Glass and polished chrome accessories add drama.
Photograph by Brian Giebelhaus

FACING PAGE TOP
Open plan interiors facilitate the West Coast lifestyle. Designer details include a curved inlaid tile pattern echoing the curved ceiling detail. Crystal chandeliers add glamour to this casual room.
Photograph by Brian Giebelhaus

FACING PAGE BOTTOM
Incorporated in the design of this project was the client's love of rich colours and architecture. This was achieved through the selection of dramatic finishes, handcrafted furnishings and original artwork.
Photograph by Samantha Dodson

JC SCOTT

JC SCOTT DESIGN ASSOCIATES

Good art paints a picture. New art defines a generation. Revolutionary art affects the planet. With an eye for design and a commitment to construct buildings that honor the Earth throughout his career, JC Scott has been blending art and functionality with green principles one project at a time. As a youth, JC was encouraged in the arts, and although he had the aptitude for a career in medicine, he chose to study art and design at Queens University, majoring in architectural history and working through school as a silversmith. JC has applied environmental solutions throughout his architectural designs, serving as a champion for the green movement as one of the first sustainable designers in British Columbia.

His awareness of wellness is integrated into a philosophy that good architecture goes beyond doing no harm and that good design is fundamental to sustaining people's health and protecting our environment. Two components that contribute to healthy designs are incorporated into every project: JC avoids toxins and harmful finishing materials like VOCs while harmoniously blending traditional design principles like Feng Shui. By creating spaces that encourage both physical and spiritual balance with the Earth, a healthy, thriving environment is produced.

Deriving much of his inspiration from nature, JC enjoys creating healthy environments that inspire creativity and says one of his favorite projects was designing a lodge and resort—Painter's Lodge. At the time, he was working mainly on nightclub designs and was chosen because the owner wanted a creative solution from an experienced hospitality designer for this upscale, out-of-city lodge that hosts sold-out annual art weekends.

ABOVE
Placed within the home beneath an open staircase is an indoor pond and waterfall accompanied by a large sculpture, *Phoenix Rising*.
Photograph by JoAnn Richards

FACING PAGE
Incorporated into the property, warm stone and cast concrete add casual elegance to this beachfront home. Hidden behind the artwork is a flat-screen television.
Photograph by Justine Murphy

Though JC is quick to say that his favorite project is his next project, a residential design stands out in his memory as particularly unique. A well-known businessman and art collector asked him to design a nearly all-glass house on a rocky point in a seismic zone. The challenge for an architectural history expert was to construct a glass house that was distinctive, especially since so many excellent glass houses by famous designers already exist. As a reflection of the home's waterfront proximity, JC brought a yacht-like approach, using curves in the spatial design. In the end, a marine-environmental house with a 360-degree view was produced through creative engineering and purposeful vision.

While his extensive portfolio of work includes custom residences and resorts, along with spas, wellness and hospitality facilities, JC has tremendous influence in the green movement through a promotional vehicle called GreenBuilt Environmental. In 1984, he was approached by a friend and a professor of environmental philosophy to start a company that promotes environmental design and responsible products including certified wood, eco-paints and finishes.

A catalyst for the green movement, JC Scott continues to lead the way in creative solutions by maintaining his unique jeweler's approach to detail for both the smallest and largest of his projects.

LEFT
Moss-green granite tops the recycled fir cabinets within this environmentally harmonious bath—both the shower and floor have a river of green glass pebbles.
Photograph by Justine Murphy

FACING PAGE
In order to create an inviting atmosphere, this guest bedroom in a landmark condominium building is capped off with pineapples—a symbol of welcome and hospitality.
Photograph by Heath Moffatt

GEELE SOROKA
THU WATSON

SUBLIME INTERIORS
TRUE WORTH REALTY

Spreading throughout Vancouver is a new approach to interior design. Thanks to professionals like Geele Soroka and Thu Watson, there's a fresh and chic ambience being applied to some of the area's most prestigious residences. Guided by the function and form of a space, Geele and Thu have built their respective firms—Sublime Interiors and True Worth Realty—with a strong commitment to innovation and style.

First and foremost, Geele and Thu know that to create an impeccable interior, they must listen to their clients with the greatest care. This sensitivity is recognized by their colleagues and the tradespeople they interact with on a daily basis. When a home is complete, it is reflective of the designer's intuition and the client's lifestyle.

Geele's style can be described as balanced—modern contemporary with an elegant twist. Clean lines and solid materials are just a few of the elements that contribute to her ever-evolving style. By pulling colours from the site's surrounding views, Geele establishes a delicate indoor-outdoor balance within her interiors.

ABOVE
A peaceful and welcoming feeling transitions between the indoor and outdoor spaces.
Photograph by Ivan Hunter Photography

FACING PAGE
With architecture by David Christopher of FX 40 Building Design Corporation, the space embraces a grand, exciting and relaxing atmosphere. A variety of shapes and textures, placed upon a neutral palette with punches of colour, add to the living room's ambience.
Photograph by Ivan Hunter Photography

One glimpse at Thu's designs reflects her innate ability to create homes with sensual elegance and distinguished taste. She pairs her creativity with carefully designed concepts and draws inspiration from around the world.

Together, Geele and Thu bring a unique experience to clients. Their expertise and accomplishments ensure homeowners that their residences are in capable, talented hands. They both thrive on the challenges each project brings and draw new inspiration from each experience. While Geele and Thu provide clear plans and guidelines for their projects, they are also aware of the benefits of flexibility. This project awareness releases an innovation that is effortlessly echoed through their individual projects and the ones they work on collaboratively.

RIGHT
Frameless glass railings capture a calm and relaxing lifestyle with breathtaking views of nature.
Photograph by Ivan Hunter Photography

FACING PAGE
Reflective materials guide visitors toward the full view from the kitchen, while also pulling the surrounding natural beauty inside.
Photograph by Ivan Hunter Photography

As accomplished professionals, they deftly combine furnishings from various cultures and design movements to produce homes that reflect a sharp judgment, adaptable approach and commitment to excellence. They instill confidence in their clients with their continuity, consistency and solid management practices.

When their mutual talents coalesce within the walls of a luxurious residence, Geele and Thu bring clarity and excellence to many of today's most stunningly contemporary homes. By sharing ideas and collective experiences, their design solutions journey beyond commonplace style and into a whole new genre.

ABOVE LEFT
This kitchen's modernity is defined by its solid gray cabinets, stainless-steel appliances and backsplash. Black granite countertops further reflect a sleek lifestyle in this West Coast home.
Photograph by Ivan Hunter Photography

ABOVE RIGHT
Upon entering the living space, guests are welcomed by a grand fireplace with rustic granite rock in contrast with a stainless steel modern fireplace surround.
Photograph by Ivan Hunter Photography

FACING PAGE TOP
In this living space the use of low furniture provides access to the view, accentuates the grand height of the space and highlights the architecture and ceiling beams.
Photograph by Ivan Hunter Photography

FACING PAGE BOTTOM
A round dining table maximizes the relaxed atmosphere for all friends and family.
Photograph by Ivan Hunter Photography

With an established rapport among their repeat clients and a well-grounded foundation in design ingenuity, Geele and Thu continue to challenge the industry's status quo and redefine the parameters of sophisticated interiors.

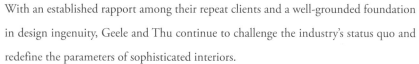

Liz Garay-Stevenson

STEVENSON DESIGN WORKS

Liz Stevenson sits at her desk, the sunshine streaming through the windows of her studio. Her desk is cluttered, papers strewn about, and as usual, she is on the phone with a client. She reaches across the desk, picks up exactly the piece of paper she is looking for, makes a few notes and then hangs up the phone—another busy day for a very busy woman.

Stevenson Design Works was founded in 1990 by Liz and her husband Les, and together they operate a design/build company that combines architectural and interior design along with full-service construction. They have been in business for more than 20 years and pride themselves with handling all aspects of a project: from architectural design, interior design to completion; they will even hire the moving company.

The company has been recognized with more than 40 Canadian Home Builders Association Awards for excellence with the Best Renovator of B.C., Best Interior Design and Best Kitchen categories. The company also won an Outstanding Achievement award in recognition of the home and interior design for the 1996 Morgan Creek Street of Dreams. Stevenson Design Works has been featured in countless magazine articles while also designing and constructing many lottery homes in British Columbia.

ABOVE
In this pealed-log, post-and-beam construction, the home's grand vaulted ceilings with windows in the front and rear allow for a spectacular view throughout the home.
Photograph courtesy of Stevenson Design Works

FACING PAGE
With wood carvings inspired by the tribes of the West Coast First Nations, this residence was the grand prize international winner of the LP Smart System home of the year from Louisiana Pacific and was also named the 2001 Pacific National Exhibition Prize Home.
Photograph courtesy of Stevenson Design Works

Known in the industry for her amazing tile, cabinet and furniture designs, Liz loves to design exactly what her clients are looking for, diligently interviewing them to discover their family lifestyle and entertaining requirements. With the vast amount of products available for home interiors, Liz's job is to show her clients the possibilities so they can make informed decisions.

Born and raised in Vancouver by parents who emigrated from Hungary, Liz began to lay the groundwork for her own education as a designer within her family's antique furniture store—she naturally has developed an artistic aptitude and a hands-on approach for interior design. Her style today is described as classic, timeless, livable, transitional and West Coast organic. Whether strolling around a local park, escaping up to the mountains or crossing the ocean, Liz believes that people enjoy the outdoors, and in turn she tries to create transparency in the transition from indoor to outdoor space—the tranquility felt in outdoor surroundings should be recreated within each home. She works diligently to ensure that the spirit of every client's interior design is reflective of his or her lifestyle and financial comfort level.

TOP LEFT
This two-toned kitchen with a blend of maple and cherry cabinets captures the essence for many cooks to work harmoniously.
Photograph by Eydis Einarsdottir, Studio 80s

BOTTOM LEFT
With custom-designed rubbed black cabinets by Lienbor Custom Cabinets, this family room provides a sanctuary where the owners can enjoy many moments together. The upper cabinets are lit to showcase the homeowners' collectables.
Photograph by Eydis Einarsdottir, Studio 80s

FACING PAGE TOP
This beautiful sun-filled room opens onto the home's pool and outdoor entertaining space. A custom area rug and rustic furniture facilitate a relaxing environment.
Photograph courtesy of Stevenson Design Works

FACING PAGE BOTTOM
A gold Georgie Award winner, this kitchen's two-tone cabinets fill the room with inspiration for all that gather here. Custom tiles and reclaimed-fir flooring are enhanced by the surrounding design elements.
Photograph courtesy of Stevenson Design Works

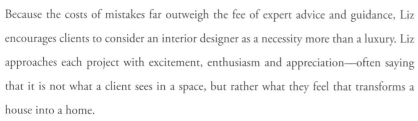

Because the costs of mistakes far outweigh the fee of expert advice and guidance, Liz encourages clients to consider an interior designer as a necessity more than a luxury. Liz approaches each project with excitement, enthusiasm and appreciation—often saying that it is not what a client sees in a space, but rather what they feel that transforms a house into a home.

ABOVE LEFT
The rich exotic tones of the walls and furnishings complement the surroundings. Entry columns and a beautiful tray ceiling welcome guests into the home.
Photograph by Eydis Einarsdottir, Studio 80s

ABOVE RIGHT
This grand foyer features custom millwork—which provides architectural detail throughout. The custom staircase and complementary wrought-iron chandelier enhance the grand entry. A custom-designed contemporary settee completes the look.
Photograph by Eydis Einarsdottir, Studio 80s

FACING PAGE TOP
Custom-designed furnishings fill the traditional library, where fabrics from Beacon Hill and a custom rug from M.R. Evans play harmoniously in the space. Custom maple millwork surrounds this space and invites guests to curl up with a good book.
Photograph courtesy of Stevenson Design Works

FACING PAGE BOTTOM
The gourmet kitchen was renovated to provide a culinary expert the opportunity to feature her skills. Alder cabinets with a dramatic countertop and stone-faced island give this kitchen the perfect amount of flair.
Photograph courtesy of Stevenson Design Works

LISA TURNER

LISA TURNER DESIGN

Desiring a career with more autonomy and creativity, Lisa Turner left the hotel industry to add a diploma of interior design to her degree in political science. As a student, she was drawn to the work of designers such as Philippe Starck, who integrates his historical European aesthetic with modern materials. As she moved forward, Lisa began to focus on precisely what homeowners value, how their lives should influence the form and function of a space. Upon graduating from Humber College in 1991, she worked for Preston's Interiors in Vancouver. Ten years and two sons later, she took a year off and began strategizing and conceptualizing the foundation of Lisa Turner Design.

Her interest in the sociology and interaction of people expanded to the foundation of how a space works. Because serious problems can often seep into a structurally disjointed home, Lisa takes great care in examining a home's layout to ensure that it is cohesive and conducive to decorative aspects.

When homeowners approached Lisa for interior design services on a penthouse they had just purchased, she looked at the home's blueprints and recognized some weaknesses in its functionality. Time and experience had taught Lisa that the home's vast, open spaces would not work in coordination with the clients' vast art collection. She advised them to incorporate new walls into the space, which allowed their art pieces to be displayed throughout the house while still maintaining an open ambience.

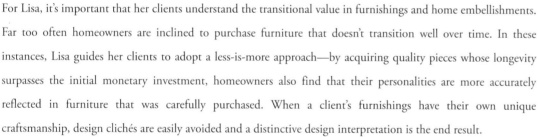

For Lisa, it's important that her clients understand the transitional value in furnishings and home embellishments. Far too often homeowners are inclined to purchase furniture that doesn't transition well over time. In these instances, Lisa guides her clients to adopt a less-is-more approach—by acquiring quality pieces whose longevity surpasses the initial monetary investment, homeowners also find that their personalities are more accurately reflected in furniture that was carefully purchased. When a client's furnishings have their own unique craftsmanship, design clichés are easily avoided and a distinctive design interpretation is the end result.

Lisa's innate curiosity about the world around her causes her designs to stand out. And to keep her inspirations fresh and aware, Lisa reads and travels frequently. By absorbing even the simplest details, she constantly expands her knowledge base to provide clients with projects that are far from the cookie-cutter mold. Responding not only to a home's particular style, Lisa considers the climate and unique qualities of the West Coast, and utilizes as much natural light as possible in her designs. And in order to achieve these distinguishable spaces, Lisa gladly relies on and interacts with local tradespeople who take her interior designs and apply their specific skills—ensuring that the end result reflects her initial concept.

ABOVE LEFT
Two tub chairs upholstered in handpainted fabric were inspired by the designs of Austrian painter Gustav Klimt and add intimacy and function to the master bedroom.
Photograph by Ed White Photographics

ABOVE RIGHT
The master ensuite's marble floors and cherry millwork complement the harmonious palette as textures unify the private and public spaces.
Photograph by Ed White Photographics

FACING PAGE
The master bedroom becomes an oasis of wood, silk and tufted leather. Views to the downtown core of Vancouver sparkle in the distance.
Photograph by Ed White Photographics

One of the most enjoyable aspects of being an interior designer is the deep level of engagement required when seeking creative solutions that are simultaneously efficient. Creating homes that are integral to her clients' lifestyles is a highlight for Lisa, who operates as the direct contact on every project. Her word is her honor, and she works at an unmatched level of professionalism with documentation that impresses her often-repeat clientele.

GREGORY VAN SICKLE

VAN SICKLE DESIGN CONSULTANTS INC

Timelessly traditional, cutting-edge contemporary or a perfect blend of the two; whole-house designs or one-room-at-a-time renovations; locales from Vancouver and Los Angeles to Umbria, London and Hong Kong. Regardless of his clients' stylistic preferences, the scope and depth of their needs or the location of their home, Gregory Van Sickle maintains that the foundations for a successful design are the same—great space planning and attention to detail. Though too humble to admit, he evolves these simple premises into brilliant designs with layer upon layer of thoughtful textures, hues and detailing that possess a collected sensibility.

The principal of Van Sickle Design Consultants has a longstanding interest in design. From a young age, he enjoyed perusing local antique shops and auction houses with his mother and recalls a particularly inspirational holiday spent in Southern California at the home of a family friend—a prominent designer of furniture and interiors. The decision to study design was natural for Gregory, who chose the Faculty of Architecture

at the University of Manitoba for his formal education and then furthered his creative pursuits by joining Robert Ledingham's legendary practice, working with London-based furniture designer Shane Glover, and then striking out on his own on Bastille Day 2000.

Gregory has a penchant for a broad range of design elements—fine art, Asian antiques and contemporary furniture, among others—and relishes each opportunity to combine his passions with those of his clients to create bespoke individual interiors.

Clients oftentimes engage in projects with only abstract notions of what they want; it is the designer's prerogative to rapidly assess design possibilities and inspire people to see their spaces in an entirely new light. The firm's principal savors nothing more than the moment clients realize the broad-reaching significance of the improvements he and his team have proposed—how the design has the potential to change their lives. He has an eye for design and achieves such masterful, strong creations through the meticulous application of textures, colour, lighting, floor and wall finishes, woodwork and furniture. Everything is created with the residents foremost in mind, so if the ideal bench, table or other piece cannot be acquired, Gregory simply drafts a design and has it crafted. If clients want their bed to be easily repositionable to take in views or enjoy the fireplace on a whim, he finds a way to surpass their expectations and create for them a one-of-a-kind environment. Avoiding repetition is a core value of his practice, so he encourages clients to think big.

It comes as no surprise that one of Gregory's favorite edicts was uttered by the venerable Mies van der Rohe: "God is in the details." There is a strong architectural dimension to all of the designer's projects; he insists in being involved both tactically and strategically in the construction planning to ensure that form and function are in perfect harmony. Ever mindful of scale, proportions and detailing, design elements are woven together in a way that allows each to be individually expressed yet blend seamlessly into the overall composition. Beautiful things combined in a balanced way—this is the essence of Van Sickle Design Consultants.

ABOVE
Eucalyptus millwork, granite and French limestone combine to create a timeless and contemporary gourmet kitchen.
Photograph by Ed White Photographics

RIGHT
A spa-like environment was the design brief for the master ensuite.
Photograph by Ed White Photographics

FACING PAGE TOP
Panoramic city and harbor views blend seamlessly with contemporary art and sculpture.
Photograph by Ed White Photographics

FACING PAGE BOTTOM
A perfect blend of custom woven carpets, handpainted fabrics, leather and mohair integrate the living area with its Stanley Park backdrop.
Photograph by Ed White Photographics

GEORGE VERDOLAGA

FLOWFORM DESIGN GROUP, LTD

George Verdolaga is part of a new breed of designers who have an international résumé of experience, are multilingual and travel constantly to keep abreast of trends. Born and raised in the Philippines, George got his interior design degree in Manila. Upon graduating, he felt a big urge to leave the comfort zone of his family and his familiar surroundings and gain experience from leading practitioners in Europe and North America.

Starting off with Sawaya and Moroni in Milan, George learned the furniture and retail side of the business. The following year, he went to New York City to work for Dorf Associates, a restaurant design firm doing projects primarily for the Walt Disney company. Returning to the Philippines to plan his next move, George worked for Litonjua & Associates, an architecture and interior design firm, before deciding on finally establishing his base in Vancouver in 1999. After enrolling with BCIT and working with several residential and commercial design firms in the city, George went on his own, establishing Flowform Design Group in 2002. Since moving to Vancouver, he has fallen in love with the city's slower pace of life.

George sees the designer's role as being threefold: fulfilling the client's vision (creative), minding deadlines and costs (managerial) and making sure the client is happy throughout the project (psychological). His painstaking attention to the details in each project means that he can only do a small number of projects each year, believing that this is the only way to ensure the highest quality and complete satisfaction on the part of the client. This particular approach has certainly won him growing recognition, as he has been asked by several of his existing clients to come back and do more work.

George feels strongly about constantly seeking new visual and interpersonal experiences to stay fresh. He also believes in the importance of continually expanding his worldview through conversation with people from different cultures and religions. And he says

ABOVE
By dividing a large space in half, the dining room now sits adjacent to the living area with a simplicity that embraces a modern Zen flavor.
Photograph by Paxton Downard

FACING PAGE
While the original plans for this heritage house included removal of the fireplace, the designer worked with the dramatic stone and incorporated red accent pieces, allowing it to function as the centerpiece of the room.
Photograph by Todd Duncan

that in order to produce something new, one must study the old. From there, one can analyze how past approaches can solve present-day problems. Citing the beauty and grandeur of Rome as an example, ancient planners had to turn to the ancient civilization of Greece for inspiration. Europe, with its historically and architecturally rich cities, is his favorite destination. Like a sponge, George absorbs everything that his senses can pick up at home and abroad such as music, language, film, pictures and text, which serve as raw material for his design thought process.

For George, the most rewarding part of his profession is being able to help people relieve their stress and tension and be more effective at home and at work by unlocking the potential in their space.

ABOVE LEFT
Seamlessly combining graceful, timeless and contemporary elements, this functional and refined dining room is made complete with a glass chandelier and polycarbonate chairs.
Photograph by Chris Lemay

ABOVE RIGHT
Desiring a relaxing area, this smart and appealing Zen transition space includes an octagonal mirror and gives a minimalist introduction with a hint of Asian influence.
Photograph by Ema Peter

FACING PAGE TOP
A nod to the owners' ethnic heritage, this living and dining room includes Philippine materials and a wooden dining table from China.
Photograph by Todd Duncan

FACING PAGE BOTTOM
This Craftsman-style house tastefully blended a retro feeling with its Gucci coffee table, 1960s' inspired couches, clean and modernist lines—ultimately creating an eclectic mix including some of the clients' art pieces.
Photograph by Ema Peter

KAREN WEST

KAREN WEST DESIGN GROUP, INC.

Typical construction language has a reputation for confusing just about anyone who hasn't spent significant time learning its intricacies. From setting trusses to draw schedules, the endless verbiage seemingly resembles a language all its own. But for Karen West, this world of construction lingo is familiar and quite normal.

Having entered the world of interior design "from the inside out" after working for a construction firm for 11 years, Karen is a valuable asset to her clients. Not only can she envision a design concept, but she can effectively translate it to the craftspeople who will actually construct the product. If she designs a waterwall, with second-nature ease she gathers measurements and estimates the total number of tiles required. Karen credits her involvement with the construction industry for giving her a good sense of creation from the core.

One of the many enjoyable aspects within the industry's varied demands is its limitless avenues within residential projects. Whether infusing a contemporary Hawaiian design into a townhome development or combining Arizona's flavors into a West Coast residence, Karen actively engages in the conceptualization of ideas and delights in crafting a project's direction. Her portfolio speaks for itself and its breadth is evident within numerous commercial and residential projects, each of which is informed by a unique life experience.

ABOVE
A West Coast contemporary bathroom features grained matte tile, riverstone accents, glass block and a vanity with wheelchair-accessible polished laminate cabinetry, four-inch thick countertop and oversized square sinks.
Photograph by J. Yanyshyn

FACING PAGE
With spectacular city and ocean views, the home's central elements are low-profile, dual holographic fireplaces. Additional aesthetics include a hexagonal recessed ceiling, iced polylaminate cabinetry and honed porcelain tiles.
Photograph by J. Yanyshyn

During her traveling excursions, Karen absorbs her surroundings; new hotels offer her a chance to capture their design concepts and perhaps incorporate certain aspects into an upcoming project. Karen's daily love for reading books and design magazines serves to refresh her design perspectives. Never does she consult a home-decorating show—after working all day with design professionals, she recognizes the need to expand her cultural and artistic knowledge.

Her design flexibility is evidenced in two of her latest projects. Karen influenced the design of a cliffside Zen retreat with a contemporary pagoda-shaped roof, floating waterwall and sleek, straight lines. At the same time, she designed a West Coast farmhouse with circular ceiling details, a combination of natural slate and stone and 12-foot waterwall replete with eight varieties of tile. While the projects are innovative and quite distinct in their design qualities, both reflect the confidence of a designer who knows how to sense her clients' personalities.

Karen West Design Group was founded in 1995 and continues in its commitment to provide professional services with a down-to-earth approach. Clients are an active ingredient in the process of defining a project's recipe—a distinctive characteristic that energizes its creative spirit. Looking beyond the fundamental necessities, Karen follows the mantra that "a vision is the art of seeing things invisible."

ABOVE
A sunken living room for mind and body relaxation is enhanced by a raised flagstone pad, large meditative stepping stones, palms, ferns, a trickling waterfall and Koi pond entrance.
Photograph by J. Yanyshyn

FACING PAGE TOP
Arched ledge stone walls encompass a built-in cooktop and its feature-wall tile accent; terrazzo tiles lead to a double-door butler's pantry.
Photograph by J. Yanyshyn

FACING PAGE BOTTOM
A great room off the kitchen showcases raised ceilings and a hand-plastered adobe fireplace within a waterfall detail, which is designed to accommodate the television and lighted art pieces.
Photograph by J. Yanyshyn

WESTERN CANADA TEAM
REGIONAL PUBLISHER: Carla Bowers
ASSOCIATE PUBLISHER: Karen Lim
SENIOR GRAPHIC DESIGNER: Emily A. Kattan
EDITOR: Amanda Bray
PRODUCTION COORDINATOR: Drea Williams

HEADQUARTERS TEAM
PUBLISHER: Brian G. Carabet
PUBLISHER: John A. Shand
EXECUTIVE PUBLISHER: Phil Reavis
DIRECTOR OF DEVELOPMENT & DESIGN: Beth Benton Buckley
DIRECTOR OF BOOK MARKETING & DISTRIBUTION: Julia Hoover
PUBLICATION MANAGER: Lauren B. Castelli
GRAPHIC DESIGNER: Jonathan Fehr
GRAPHIC DESIGNER: Ashley Rodges
EDITORIAL DEVELOPMENT SPECIALIST: Elizabeth Gionta
MANAGING EDITOR: Rosalie Z. Wilson
EDITOR: Katrina Autem
EDITOR: Anita M. Kasmar
EDITOR: Ryan Parr
EDITOR: Daniel Reid
MANAGING PRODUCTION COORDINATOR: Kristy Randall
PRODUCTION COORDINATOR: Laura Greenwood
TRAFFIC COORDINATOR: Amanda Johnson
TRAFFIC COORDINATOR: Meghan Anderson
ADMINISTRATIVE MANAGER: Carol Kendall
ADMINISTRATIVE ASSISTANT: Beverly Smith
CLIENT SUPPORT COORDINATOR: Amanda Mathers
CLIENT SUPPORT ASSISTANT: Aimee Beresford

PANACHE PARTNERS, LLC
CORPORATE HEADQUARTERS
1424 Gables Court
Plano, TX 75075
469.246.6060
www.panache.com

Zebra Design & Interiors Group, *page 69*

Index

THE PANACHE COLLECTION

Dream Homes Series
An Exclusive Showcase of the Finest Architects, Designers and Builders

Carolinas
Chicago
Coastal California
Colorado
Deserts
Florida
Georgia
Los Angeles
Metro New York
Michigan
Minnesota

New England
New Jersey
Northern California
Ohio & Pennsylvania
Pacific Northwest
Philadelphia
South Florida
Southwest
Tennessee
Texas
Washington, D.C.

Spectacular Homes Series
An Exclusive Showcase of the Finest Interior Designers

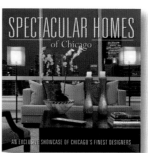

California
Carolinas
Chicago
Colorado
Florida
Georgia
Heartland
London
Michigan
Minnesota
New England

New York
Ohio & Pennsylvania
Pacific Northwest
Philadelphia
South Florida
Southwest
Tennessee
Texas
Toronto
Washington, D.C.
Western Canada

Perspectives on Design Series
Design Philosophies Expressed by Leading Professionals

Carolinas
Chicago
Colorado
Florida
Georgia
Minnesota

New England
Pacific Northwest
San Francisco
Southwest
Texas

City by Design Series
An Architectural Perspective

Atlanta
Charlotte
Chicago
Dallas
Denver
Orlando
Phoenix
San Francisco
Texas

Spectacular Wineries Series
A Captivating Tour of Established, Estate and Boutique Wineries

California Central Coast
Napa Valley
New York
Sonoma

Art of Celebration Series
The Making of a Gala

Florida Style
New York Style
Washington, D.C. Style

Specialty Titles

Distinguished Inns of North America
Extraordinary Homes California

Spectacular Golf of Colorado
Spectacular Golf of Texas
Spectacular Hotels

Spectacular Restaurants of Texas
Visions of Design

Panache Partners, LLC   1424 Gables Court   Plano, Texas 75075   469.246.6060   www.panache.com